MW01699916

Traveling Solo

The Only Overseas Economy Travel Guide for Women

by

Shalla Callahan

Callahan Castle Publishing
Long Beach, California

Published and distributed in the United States by
Callahan Castle Publishing
264 Lowena Drive, Long Beach, CA 90803

This book is designed to provide information relating to the subject matter covered. It is sold with the understanding that the publisher and author are not engaged in rendering legal or professional services. If expert assistance is required, the services of a competent professional should be sought. The purpose of this book is to educate and entertain. The author and publisher will have neither liability nor responsibility to any person or entity with respect to any loss or damage caused, or alleged to be caused, directly or indirectly by any information contained in this book. Every effort has been made to make this book as complete and accurate as possible. However, there may be mistakes both typographical and in content. Therefore, this text should be used only as a general guide and not as the ultimate source of travel information and contains information only up to the printing date. If you do not wish to be bound by this, you may return this book for a full refund.

Some of the information contained in this book may not be deemed politically correct. It is not meant to offend but is merely one woman's depiction of her experiences in particular countries. Most if not all of the malfeasance appeared to be committed by the males in these societies and seldom if ever were women felt to be a threat. Even in the USA today, if a dog is purchased for protection it is seldom to guard against females. Every day, headlines around the world are filled with mostly male violence and it is this author's opinion that our tax structure should be modified to reflect this disparity. " Why should women be equally responsible for paying the cost of male crime in a society that feels justified in paying women less money for equal work? Examples abound of injustices to women in our so-called civilized and progressive society today and until we join together to create a more loving and enlightened world we will continue living in an unprincipled and unjust society where women are abused and devalued."

ISBN 0-9651513-5-2

Printed in the United States of America

Acknowledgments:

After struggling along for over four years trying to create this book without a computer, I took my good friend Charlie Cornett's advice and bought one. She chose it and set it up and without her help and advice I would probably still be limping along. My friend's Debbie Fank and Glen Goodlove were kind enough to type everything out on their computers until I got one and I'm sure it must have been a bit of a drag. But here it is, and even I can hardly believe it's truly completed. Another good friend, Robin Smith, is doing the cover with me and this should be fun. We traded nights at my mountain cabin for the cost of it. Sonna Elliott helped edit it and women everywhere said they wanted a copy when it was finished so this spurred me on.

My thanks to all of you. And to those who find help and humor and the courage to travel alone on a shoestring, my joyful gratitude. Goddesses all. I love you.

Table of Contents

"The mind is like an elastic band. The more you pull, the more it stretches."
-Paramahansa Yogananda

Introduction

Are you of an age to recall when occupations for women were limited to nursing, teaching, home making, secretarial work and flight attending? Not that there's anything wrong with these professions, it's just that we were limited to such few options. These were *all* the options. And if we weren't married by age twenty-one, women were labeled " old maids". Or if we weren't pregnant within two years of marriage we were looked at askance by well meaning family members and perhaps asked personal or embarrassing questions. You might be too young to have experienced this and perhaps have only heard of it from your Mother or Grandmother but let me assure you that what she tells you is true. Such a repressed plight existed for women here in the United States and currently persists in most third world countries even today. Women worldwide currently earn 30 to 40 percent less than men for comparable work and American women ages 25 to 34 earn 83 cents to a man's dollar. And even though the value of women remains so low today that a man can legally beat and kill us, as evidenced by recent court cases, in the United States things *are* getting better and more women than ever are venturing beyond societies constraints into every conceivable occupation and into the world at large.

In 1995 single Americans numbered *ninety three million* and growing. Well over half that number are female and in the past five years over *five million* Americans traveled alone. Not only are single Western women found in every avenue of today's work-place, she's exploring all corners of the globe, manifesting her unique rhythmic power and nurturing presence in the world. We are these women. Reaching out. Striving. Stretching and succeeding in making our presence known.

Aware that I had traveled extensively alone, female friends were phoning to inquire where they should travel and how...how to be safe, what to take, where to buy tickets, and dozens of questions it would have been impossible to answer in a phone conversation or even over lunch... all the intricate details of overseas solo female travel. So when it was suggested that I write a book on the subject, I felt excited not merely at the thought of filling a need but of achieving it through doing two things I feel passionate about: writing and traveling. But I felt inadequate. To make a travel book viable I needed to explore more countries. So I've spent the past several years doing just that: traveling and writing this book. It's been a long birth process but here it is. I hope you find it helpful. I would enjoy receiving comments, suggestions or updates. The one thing that's most constant is change. Even whole countries change due to economic and political trends so if you have more recent knowledge or new ideas that would help future women travelers such as yourself, I would be delighted to hear from you and possibly include the information in future guide books.

This guide book was expressly created for you . . .to help you explore exotic locations inexpensively on your own. But more than that, it takes a look at the psychological prospect of solo traveling as well. For if travel has meaning and significance it's that we are made to lift our eyes from our own existence to the whole complex magnificent world. At least once in her lifetime a woman should feel the pulsing sense of expansion and autonomy that traveling the world alone imparts. Breathing in the radiant kaleidoscopic sights, symphonic sounds and aromatic fragrance of Mother Earth chasms the soul. Exposed to educationally exhilarating cultures you may discover a hungry curiosity, a self reliant inner assurance and expansive awareness not generally experienced in the company of others. i.e. alone.

The original meaning of the word "alone" was "all one" as in "completely oneself". Today the dictionary also offers "matchless", "unequaled", "unparalleled". Solitude extends the opportunity to intrinsically know ourselves independent of our usual environ, while traveling the world alone presents us with a backdrop of incredible cultures where we can experiment with new and exciting ways of being and relating in the world.

The following are just a few of the countless reasons for traveling alone:

1. You're gloriously free to change your mind about anything at any given moment.
2. You don't have to adjust to anyone's schedule. Eat and explore anytime, anyplace.
3. People open up and socialize more with a person traveling alone.
4. You're more likely to be invited to stay in someone's home should you feel so inclined.
5. Wake and sleep on your own time clock.
6. Friends at home may think of you in a particular way. Traveling alone opens up the opportunity to explore all aspects of the total You.
7. Stay longer or leave earlier without asking.
8. You'll extend yourself more, meeting extraordinary travelers from many different countries as well as colorful locals.
9. Last-minute plane tickets are much easier to obtain for one.
10. If your life at home is hectic, it's the perfect opportunity to relax and wind down.
11. Be alone or with someone; the choice is yours. You're not "stuck" with anyone. If habits of a person you've met are annoying, simply say "goodbye."
12. Locals may ask to show you their village, home, or their particular favorite sight if you're alone.
13. If you're hitch-hiking, it's easier to catch a ride.
14. When booking transportation or entertainment, better seating is more likely for one.
15. You'll make fewer compromises with your time and money and be more inclined to learn the language.
16. Finding a friend from home to travel with who has your exact travel time frame can be difficult if not impossible.
17. You're with someone you truly like...yourself, and you can pamper yourself as much as you like.
18. You may feel more assertive, alive, and in control, more self confident and vibrant than ever before.
19. You're able to look at the Earth from many angles and concentrate wholly on a particular landscape and culture with fewer distractions.

Dining where the locals dine and lodging in economy dwellings you'll encounter a more culturally authentic environment than if you occupied or dined in ordinary tourist hotels. Colorful locals, as well as entertaining and accomplished travelers seem to appear at every byway. Discover what these fascinating people do, how they live, who they are and what motivates them. Most are delighted to chat, to tell you about their country and learn about yours. Traveling solo you're more likely to meet dynamic people all over the world, natives and travelers alike and become friends, expanding one another's concepts.

Tourists permeate first class accommodations and a vast difference exists between a tourist and a traveler. A tourist is protected from the culture of a country by a glass bubble of status and wealth which separates her from the locals who end up being her maids and servants rather than her friends. A traveler absorbs infinitely more and delves far deeper into the culture by giving up the charade of class. Additionally she learns more by staying in unique and usually unassuming accommodations, eating at colorful regional cafes, and frequenting the distinctive establishments patronized by the locals for entertainment and relaxation. So all in all you'll experience a journey par excellence and at the same time, curtail expenses by socializing with local people. Hitchhiking through New Zealand's lush green hills, ominous black clouds threatening to dump buckets of rain on my head, a family- packed station wagon gave me a lift to their "Aunties" for hot tea and scones. It was a memorable time for all of us as we spread thick clotted cream on the hot scones and spoke at length of our individual countries. In Thailand I performed secretarial work for a gracious Baptist Missionary and his lovely wife who invited me to stay in their exotic teakwood home. We canoed up marshy serpentine rivers into primitive native villages where Caucasians are rarely seen. Intrigued, the natives timidly touched our white skin as we distributed vitamins and prayed. That was 19 years ago and I never miss the chance to see these dear friends whenever I'm in Thailand.

Waiting in airports can be boring, but not if you find someone interesting to talk with. In Nepal I conversed with a man waiting for the same Nepal/New Delhi flight as me. Just last month I received news of the birth of their first child, a daughter, and two years prior the three of us toured Disneyland on their first visit to the USA. I see them every time I'm in New Delhi. There's never-ending stories of all the incredibly wonderful people encountered in traveling solo and I would love to hear from you after you begin your own marvelous journey. You'll have an opportunity to form remarkable friendships and experience life in a powerful, defining way traveling solo.

In Yugoslavia I met a woman who spoke five languages. She was an attorney defecting from war torn Romania leaving behind her job, her friends and family, her husband and precious five year old daughter. Do we appreciate our Country and our freedom enough? Hajnel was willing to risk everything for something you and I were born into. I feel lucky I met her. The whole experience really opened my eyes and might not have happened had I been traveling with someone. But being alone, my time and my decisions were exclusively my own. She believed her chances of being captured would be diminished if I traveled with her so we journeyed by train through the lush majestic hills of Yugoslavia, Czechoslovakia and Hungary. I consider myself incredibly fortunate to have encountered the remarkable beauty of Yugoslavia before the war broke out and, conversely, deeply saddened knowing this breathtaking area is now destroyed. Two weeks later I smuggled food and clothing to Hajnel's family in Romania just prior to the tyrant Ceausescu's downfall and had the privilege of giving oranges to children who had never tasted them. Their eyes danced with joy as the juice dripped down their little chins and it sends a shudder through my body knowing what men do for power, how they ravage and alter lives without a thought.

While biking the pot-holed dirt roads of Kathmandu, Nepal I met a young German woman who also rented a bike and we pedaled through the dusty fascinating city and into a neighboring more sedate temple town. Exploring Nepal together we were continually laughing at life's absurdities . Two months later while traveling through Germany I stayed in her home. We sipped rich woodsy wine in her vine-covered cottage in the hills of central Germany, munched on fried Camembert cheese with mint jelly and explored local villages. Just last week I received a wedding announcement from her!

You'll learn infinitely more traveling on a shoestring. You'll have adventures unobtainable on group tours and best of all, you'll form your own world-wide lifelong friendships and a powerful independent sense of self as you are able to “conquer the world”. If someone had accompanied me on my travels it’s unlikely any of the experiences I’ve related plus dozens I haven’t mentioned, would have occurred. If someone had told me I would be singing songs with a group of farm workers on a tiny island in the South Pacific (one jolly toothless little lady was playing spoons, a young man in dungarees had a flute and another in traditional Tahitian skirt plucked the banjo), I’d have thought they were a little nuts. Of if someone had said I would be in India playing a game of Scrabble in English with native Indians who were more proficient than I, I’d have thought they were unbalanced. But anything’s possible. EVERYTHING’s possible! All you have to do is *begin.* The majority of women who have traveled alone wouldn’t do it any other way. The good and the bad, the highs and the lows, all combine to create a perfectly exquisite experience worth remembering forever. Are you ready? O.K. Here we go . . .

Venturing Forth

"Broad, wholesome, charitable views of men and things cannot be acquired by vegetating in one little corner of the earth all one's lifetime."

-Mark Twain

To begin, make a list of all the countries you've ever wanted to see. Sit back restfully in a comfortable chair, legs uncrossed, arms relaxed, and eyes gently closed. Breathe slowly and deeply, allowing names of exotic locales to drift into your mind. Visualize. Do you see swaying emerald palms, luminous white capped waves lapping at lazy softsand beaches, or languid aquamarine lakes, blazing vermillion deserts, mighty arcane pyramids, commanding snow-capped mountains, or towering ancient castles? Write down everything that flashes into your mind...no limitations. Now put this paper aside for awhile feeling free to add to it at any time, any moment day or night. Keep pen and paper by your bed in case, like me, you have late night creative ideas.

Which season appeals to you most? Do you prefer summery, sultry, warm weather climates, winter's chill crisp air or something in between? Packing is considerably lighter and you can be decidedly freer, more spontaneous and flexible in sunny weather. A heavy coat and boots can easily fill a small suitcase. An option, however, is to mail winter clothes home when leaving a cold country. I found myself in humid Southeast Asia with a Can't-Resist-It's-Sooo-Cheap ticket to Greece in dead of winter. I arrived , freezing in my flip-flops and short-sleeved T-shirt. Hugging myself to keep my teeth from chattering I wandered down the winding cobblestone street to the nearest store and purchased a woolly sheepskin coat which I mailed home from Switzerland two weeks later and years later, sold in a neighborhood garage sale for $10.00. But for all-around ease of traveling and safety, for being light, breezy and footloose, warm climates are unequaled.

Don't get too caught up in having everything perfect. Have fun! Make planning the adventure an adventure in itself. You'll soon be *traveling*, experiencing the magical intoxication of each unique moment. It could just be the finest, most blissful time you've had in your life. You're taking *exceptional* care of yourself and for those of us who always take care of others, this in itself can be an exciting adventure, an enlightening experience of the perfect and total You . Coming home means returning to work and routine so while you're free grab life by the tail and dance! Breath deeply of being alive and experience the world's most enchanting cultures, her people, animals and landscapes.

My latest trip lasted six months and the first two weeks home were dreadful. My tummy ached so badly I thought I was developing an ulcer. I wanted to leave the pressure, turn around and rush back. Dealing with all the minor hassles here we don't realize what a whirlwind pace we're in. I'm not saying that it isn't wonderful here. I cherish every mountain, every beach, every blade of grass. But the pace is fast. We live fast and hard and it's so complex. So with everything you do to get ready for this journey, whether it's a week, two weeks, or six months, have fun. Make it work and play combined. When you're following your heart, work and play flow into one another. Work becomes fun. And it's not as daunting as it may seem. The scariest thing is fear of the unknown, and after arriving it's known, so the fear vanishes. Leaving home may seem frightening at first. That's only natural. Like "a snail being pulled off your rock" to quote Anne Morrow Lindberg. Just observe it, relax, and let it go because you're going to have an exhilarating time. "Do the thing you fear and the death of fear is a certainty." Ralph Waldo Emerson.

What happens if you find yourself in a country you don't like? Give it a day or two. If it still feels uncomfortable, just leave. No one is stopping you; it's your decision and yours alone because you have the distinct benefit of traveling solo. But chances are you'll love it so much you'll want to stay even longer than planned. If not, just leave. Imagine if you were traveling with someone who wanted to stay. You'd be in a dilemma and possibly have a confrontation.

What happens if you want to stay longer than your visa permits? Just go to the nearest neighboring country, get your visa extended, return and check out job availability (assuming you want to work). In most countries you can work "under the table jobs". Numerous opportunities exist. In Australia I snorkeled the Great Barrier reef on a small yacht for three days. At the end of the voyage the Captain invited a few of us to stay on and work in the kitchen or teach snorkeling. Some travelers had been doing this for months. Countless inventive ways are available to make money and even if you don't need the cash, how about the experience? In New Zealand, parts of Europe and Australia working in the economy hotels can be an excellent way to meet people and cover expenses. It's especially easy to find jobs on bulletin boards in hostels. In Japan teaching English is popular and pays remarkably well. Explore what interests you and follow your heart. Someone once said "If you do what you love, money will follow."

A few useful books for working overseas are: *International Jobs—Where They Are, How to Get Them* and *Study and Teaching Opportunities Abroad: Sources of Information about Overseas Study, Teaching, Work and Travel.* Both are sold by International Studies, 777 United Nations Plaza, Suite 9A, New York, NY 10017. A yearly catalog of salaried but unskilled jobs in Asia, Europe and Africa is *Working Holidays* from the Canadian Bureau for International Education, 141 Leerier West, Ottawa, Ontario, Canada KIP 5J3. *Overseas List: Opportunities for Living and Working in Developing Countries* by Beckmann and Donnelly and published by Bread for the World Educational Fund, 207 E. 16th Street New York, NY 10003 is good and all are excellent if you want to work legally in a foreign country.

So stay as long as you like, have fun planning this adventure and remember, success isn't determined by material possessions. It's far deeper than that and can only be measured by inner peace and harmony, the result of knowing and loving yourself so you can then know and love others.

Shangri-la to Paradise

I am fevered with the sunset,
I am fretful with the bay
For the wander-thirst is on me
Any my soul is in Cathay"
-Richard Hovey

This book is principally geared toward women traveling on a budget to foreign ports. However, if you consider Hawaii an exotic port, and indeed it *is* a tropical paradise, the least expensive route to Hawaii can be found in your local newspaper's Sunday travel section. If there isn't anything exciting in your paper send for or go to your local news stand and purchase the Sunday *L. A. Times* from California. In the travel section you'll find sensational bargains to the Islands. If you're visiting only Oahu, this is the one place you should purchase your flight in conjunction with accommodations for maximum value. It's possible to get a car thrown into the bargain but the bus in Hawaii is inexpensive so if it comes down to a choice between a car or hotel, take the hotel. Ride the bus around Oahu for $.60, slightly uncomfortably. For those who aren't especially daring, Hawaii's a tenable first-time solo adventure . . . the monetary system's the same (of course), everyone speaks English, and you're still in the United States. But Hawaii can feel somewhat romantic with tropical air and the scent of plumaria blossoms wafting through the air. If you can handle that then you'll do fine on these lovely mostly-safe islands. But if you weren't adventurous, you probably wouldn't be reading this book would you. So let's get a bit daring and more exotic.

For the woman who's only somewhat anxious traveling by herself, I recommend countries where English is well spoken, such as the British Isles, New Zealand, Australia, and Singapore. But I've found people all over the globe who speak passable to marginal English. We're very fortunate in this way. So my personal favorite trip for impetuously brave kindred spirits is a Southeast Asian or South Pacific loop. There's simply more variety here at better prices than anywhere else in the world. It's safe, the food is delicious, the people are friendly and you can live like a Queen for a pittance. Purchase a ticket starting in Bangkok. Thailand may have more visible historical evidence of past cultures than any other South-East Asian country if you're at all interested in ruins, temples, Buddhas, Kings and Queens, orange-robed monks, and early civilizations. Take a water taxi from the airport into town for an amazing and picturesque view of life on the waterways and see all the amazing sights Bangkok offers. If you hunger for diversity, pungent smells, astounding sights, clattering sounds and foreign intrigue, then Bangkok might be your city. You'll encounter incredible aromas and curious spectacles as you walk through bustling markets and down dusty clamorous streets, congested, jostling, reeking and frenetic; absolutely fascinating. People ask why women tour Thailand, there's such an aura of sensuality and sex. Instead of saying "will you?", it's "why won't you?" but it's an attitude, a different set of values. And in a few third world countries women do what they must to survive. It is however, considered one of Thailand's major problems and AIDS is taking its toll. But Bangkok isn't all of Thailand by any means.

Witness the splendor of lush verdant islands jutting out of crystalline radiant seas. Craggy majestic vine covered cliffs plunge into velvety sand beaches to the South while charming picturesque villages and colorful psychedelic hill tribes inhabit the North. When you're sick of the traffic and pollution in Bangkok, hop on a train and ride up to the hill tribes in the North with an overnight stay at Kanchanaburi on the way. Spend a leisurely day floating down the legendary River Kwai on an all-you-can-eat fruit laden bamboo barge and explore the ancient esoteric Buddhist caves . . . all for a whopping $2. Here you can stay in a bamboo hut on the river's edge with a view of the famous bridge for $3.00. Thoroughly explored, you'll leave your heart but not your pocketbook in Thailand. After riding an elephant in the lush steamy jungles in the North and exploring Chaing Mai and the fascinating hill tribes, take the train South to the loveliest little islands I've seen in my life. Kho Phi Phi just South of Krabi by boat is one of my favorites with crystal waters and jagged vine covered cliffs. Phangnga's pristine beaches and swaying palms has much to recommend it too. Over night trains are clean, comfortable, inexpensive, and serve tasty food. Ride clear to the Malaysian border where you'll find the island of Penang which I don't find especially intriguing but lots of people do. It's the oldest British settlement on the Malay Peninsula and has some nice beaches, interesting temples, a Chinese clan house, and good food. Back on the train, continue down to Tapah and catch the bus ride up to the Cameron Highlands. It's quite a winding spectacular trip with vines the size of elephant trunks overhanging the narrow road. Once there, trek the lush tropical rain forests. This is possibly the most extensive and best known hill stations in South East Asia with thousands of butterflies and pleasantly cool weather. Taman Negara is Malaysia's National Park where a ride upriver means stepping into a world where little has changed in the last 130 million years! A protected forest reserve where many rare and endangered species can still be found, this is the oldest rainforest on earth. On the train heading South once more (Malaysia is a long finger of land stretching down to Singapore) hop off at the capital of Kuala Lumpur which the British made their Malayan capital in the tin mining days. Today it's a spectacularly beautiful progressive skyscrapered city that's easy to traverse with lots to see. Even the train station is a lovely sight and although KL is Malaysia's largest city, it's population is barely over one million.

Down the entire Malaysian peninsula you'll be passing miles and miles of palm trees which of course is why palm oil is one of Malaysia's biggest exports along with tin and rubber. Sights from the train are tantamount to the best Disney ride you'll ever be on and my personal favorite way to travel. You can walk around, stretch, or go to the dining car while the surrounding panorama of breathtaking mountains, villages, bridges and rivers, street scenes, valleys, and sunsets rolls slowly by . And all the while, the gentle click clack rocking is transporting you nearer your next tantalizing adventure.

This time it's the spic and span, shoppers' paradise, garden-like, civilized island of Singapore. The most affluent country in Asia besides Japan, your luggage will be sniffed for drugs by dogs when you arrive at the train station. Everyone speaks English, and everything is so clean and orderly you can drink water from the tap and enjoy Asia's best gourmet food at reasonable prices. The food's sumptuously exotic, especially at the not to be missed food hawker stalls. Walk the streets safely in the balmy night air and shop till you drop for everything from electronics to kid skin hand-stitched shoes. Singapore is unquestionably the most organized country in Asia. With its glistening streets (tossing a cigarette butt on the ground can warrant a $200 fine), shimmering skyscrapers and superb shopping malls, it's a mixture of archaic and avant-garde, contemporary yet ancient, fashionable yet obsolete . . . more civilized than most. Stay in the YMCA at the bottom of Orchard Road for under $15 with air conditioning. You may want to get reservations ahead if you know when you'll be there but if the Y is full there are other economical accommodations around town in the Bencoolen area. Just shop around. The YWCA just up the hill is ancient and pretty, surrounded by huge lovely draping shade trees.

Singapore is a good place to buy inexpensive flights to other destinations. I always purchase my ticket to Bali in Singapore with a stop-over in Java on the way. And Singapore's Changi Airport is almost as beautiful as Hawaii's. The city bus is the cheapest and best way to get to or from the airport but taxis are reasonable too and you won't be cheated. Then it's off to Java and Bali. You'll know when you're entering Indonesia by the sweet pungent aroma of clove cigarettes wafting through the misty tropical air and the gracious smiling faces of the natives. In Java rent a bike and ride around Jakarta and Yogyakarta for an educational look at the culture. Java has both wealth and squalor and good food and accommodations are available at incredibly affordable prices. Visit the superb Mt. Bromo volcano and the various temples if you aren't "templed-out" by now. For more peaceful surroundings head on down to Bali. Away from the clamor of the city, one returns to joy in simple things. In Bali there are no television sets or movie theaters to distract you so the opportunity exists to be incredibly in touch with yourself. The great philosopher and scientist Pasquelle once said that all problems stem from the inability to sit quietly in a room alone. The Balinese are delighted to have you in their country and relish the opportunity to visit with Americans. Kuta is primarily Australians as they're able to fly to Bali for a fraction of what it costs to travel the vast distances in their own country and Kuta is nicknamed "Little Australia". Not that that's bad; it's interesting. But if you want to explore Bali, limit your time in Kuta with its' touristy prices. The rest of Bali will enchant you. Musical, magical Bali. If green is your favorite color and Spring is your preferred season, then Bali is your Shangri La...a tropical island so immaculate and picturesque you may never want to leave. The people live, breathe and die for art, music and religion and the island is a plethora of terraced rice paddies, temples, warm water streams, brightly colored flowers and smiling faces. It's about $129 to catch a round trip ticket to Bali from Singapore and well worth the time if you avoid their rainy season which is incredibly hot and muggy. In the busy capital city of Denpassar taxi drivers will attempt to whisk you down to Kuta Beach which I don't recommend except for, perhaps, one day on the seashore witnessing the breath-taking sunset, shopping, and socializing with the Australians. Put on your bikini and be lulled into oblivion with a massage on the sand for $2. In Thailand the same experience is attainable and in my opinion the Thais are the best masseuses in the world stretching your limbs and torso into pretzels. If you want privacy a massage in a hotel spa is about $12 an hour. But back to Bali...if you miss Kuta altogether you won't be missing much.

Candidasa, a picturesque Balinese beach village has thirst quenching fresh fruit juices and sun drenched beaches to lie on, while Ubud, the main art center in Bali, is nestled in the cooler, lush, rice terraced mountains and a must on anyone's agenda. It's here one can escape the passionate tropical heat, explore the mystical monkey forest and investigate local artists' wares or foreign artists in residence like Hans Snel or the Spanish artist Blanco. Walk down the main road to the suspension bridge for a truly lush picturesque sight (don't forget your camera), eat some black rice pudding with bananas at Murni's then cross the bridge and stop in Begar's Bush for a drink, a game, Cajun music, creamy chocolate ice cream or just great socializing. This is my favorite tavern in the world and I don't generally frequent taverns. To compare prices and quality , shop around extensively before purchasing items to take home. My favorite items to buy in Bali are clothes, leather products, wood carvings and just *exquisite* jewelry. If you ride the buses (called bemos) be wary of pickpockets and at a beach or pool in any country don't leave valuables lying about. Watertight pouches are available in sporting goods stores if you need one.

On your way to South East Asia why not see Hong Kong for about $100 more airfare. On your way home a stop in Hawaii is about $50 or, it could be free. Ask. If you have the time, I'd recommend it. You'll be on your own regarding accommodations in Hawaii since you don't have a package fare so check out the airport bulletin board where you'll find medium priced hotels (compared to our U.S.A. standards) for about $45 with free phones to each. If you want a B&B check the yellow pages in the phone book. There's also a YMCA conveniently located in Waikiki.

Hong Kong is a shoppers paradise and this is one place you definitely need reservations at one of the YMCAs or YWCAs before arriving. It's so overpopulated I once shared a room with a rat (the four-legged variety). I've stayed in numerous accommodations in Hong Kong and find the Y's to be the best value by far. The Y's inexpensive restaurants have nourishing meals with your choice of British or Chinese cuisine. Eat at the night market near the ferry if you're adventurous and be sure to stroll the pathway at the top of the tram for a spectacular view of the magnificent harbor and city in daylight or dark. Go up just before sunset and watch the twinkling lights of the city light up the night sky. And if you want anything custom made like silk suits or snake skin boots or shoes, Hong Kong is the place.

Just West of Hong Kong is the tiny Portuguese island of Macau, easily gotten to by ferry if you're so inclined. Rent a bike or hop on a bus to explore this historical territory. It's priced about the same as Hong Kong and sells antiques and handicrafts and has buzzing casinos where people can stand behind you and bet on your playing. A little unnerving if you ask me but I tried it anyway. Macau is the closest I've been to mainland China. Would I recommend it? Only if you have extra time and money. Tahiti is beautiful but profusely overpriced compared to South East Asia. Lunch is $30 and T-shirts are $25. Bali, Southern Thailand, and Malaysia are incredibly affordable and just as spectacular and the locals are more affable and welcoming than the Tahitians. Perhaps it's the French influence and the fact that France taxes them heavily with little compensation, but whatever it is, if you do venture to Tahiti, take lots of money and a thick skin and don't photograph the citizens unless you're prepared to be yelled at. Their religious beliefs suggest that a picture captures the spirit and is taken away in the camera. From the main village in Papeete, hop on the ferry to Morea. For $5, the ferry ride is the best bargain you'll find in Tahiti. I met a crusty little 78 year old American lady on the ferry and we hitch hiked together. She had an enormous suitcase so she'd hide in the bushes and when a vehicle would stop she'd pop out and off we'd go. We also rode the bus but her suitcase was a pain and we had different ideas about what we wanted to see so we parted company. That, of course, is a benefit when traveling alone; be with or without whomever. See what you want, whenever. If you're wealthy, fly to Bora Bora and stay in the darling water bungalows on stilts. I haven't done this myself but I've seen pictures and have heard from numerous sources that it's great.

If you love to snorkel or scuba dive, the Fijian Islands might be your cup of tea. There's not much in the way of shopping and there's some racial tension between the indigenous Fijian and the Indian settler...the main occupants of this lovely group of islands, but the white sand beaches and crystal aquamarine water are beautiful. Viti levu is the largest island and easily gotten around in a couple of days. Spend a night in Nadi, a night in Vidi levu and a night on one of the little off shore islands and you've pretty much seen it. I had a hard time getting truthful answers if my question was related to money, and the sail boat to one of the islands neglected to put my suitcase on board for the sail back to Vidi. They insisted it was in the hold but I hoped off and found it myself still on the island. New Zealand is a singularly breathtaking trip for a first time traveler. It's very much what The United States was twenty or thirty years ago only costlier . . . remarkably unspoiled and relatively safe. You can even hitch hike if you're so inclined but it might be safer if you find someone to hitch with as the world's economic trend has affected things in New Zealand like everywhere else in the world. I hitch hiked alone and had no problem but in Greymouth on the South Island someone stole my suitcase right out of my room. I bought clothes and another suitcase at the Good Will store as clothes and essentials are costly in

New Zealand but a lot of what was stolen was irreplaceable. The people are friendly and welcoming, however, and the cuisine is nourishing. It's not cheap, but it's possible to tour this dreamy fertile land on a medium budget. At the Auckland Airport, walk down to the hotel board where you'll find drivers with vans to transport you to their economy lodgings. These are generally quieter and friendlier than youth hostels, are privately run, and have happy communal kitchens . . . lively, interesting places to stay with no age limit, no curfew and no chores to do as in youth hostels. . . splendid for meeting other travelers. They also have informative bulletin boards with tons of information from miscellaneous available jobs to various bargain side trips, cars for sale, rides to share and exciting local entertainment. The kiwis (pet name for New Zealanders) couldn't be more congenial. Friendly faces are everywhere along with invitations to homes and entertainment. And the travelers you'll meet in the lodgings are as fun and friendly as the locals. It's marvelous fun socializing with all these terrific people.

Australia is comparable to New Zealand and Singapore in that it too is civilized and would combine well to create a thrilling South Pacific loop. One difficulty with Australia, however, is the huge expanse from one region to another. One bus trip from Brisbane to Cairns is eighteen hours long. A bit tiring to the derriere. The Gold Coast is broad fleecy white beaches dotted with quaint burgs where biking, surfing and luxuriating in the noonday sun consumes the day. Do be careful though, as the ozone layer here is acutely thin. Rub on #15 or higher sunscreen.

The outback is a shimmering red, arid territory, sparsely populated, comprised of yawning ancient caves, odd rock formations, and Old West townships where the pub is the gathering place for a frosty pint of beer at lunch and after work. Then explore the succulent Australian jungle, bristling with wild life and all varieties of lush vegetation. Or snorkel the Great Barrier Reef for the most dazzling experience of your life. It's the largest and oldest living organism on the earth, brilliant in color and sensational to view. I like lying very still on top of the water, snorkel in mouth, and viewing the sea's treasures moving beneath me. On my first trip to Australia I bought a terrific package trip I found on a bulletin board at one of the backpacker accommodations in Cairns. It included three days in the jungle, three in the outback and three on the Barrier Reef for under $200 which is a great deal in Australia or New Zealand but would be considered outrageously expensive in Thailand, Malaysia, or Bali. Back on shore, shopping's a blast at the two quaint flea markets in Sydney. Australia wasn't a place I particularly wanted to see but it was a possible stop on my South Pacific loop. Now I go whenever I can. It's fabulous. If you have the money, do it. If not, stick to South-East Asia.

In most countries the best sights are free. Tourist bureaus will furnish maps and lists of places of interest. Churches, temples, synagogues, museums, university campuses, parks, beaches, parades, festivals, treks, flea markets, and outdoor concerts are generally all free. And don't miss New Delhi's government buildings, Europe's spectacular architecture, Bali's vibrant burial ceremonies, Thailand's delectable floating markets or New Zealand's magnificent fjords . . . all without charge. Visit vineyards and wineries, street fairs and recreation areas, tropical rain forests and terraced rice paddies. All free.

England's a favorable country for the woman who has capital but doesn't care for language barriers. And while you're at it, why not see Scotland, Wales and Ireland? Take the train or rent a car. England isn't economical, but it's quite safe for a first time, single traveler on her own. Magnificent museums, imposing historical buildings and dazzling theater abound. I stayed in a fairly clean, unobtrusive B&B near Victoria Station for $25 a night and eagerly managed to see nine plays in two weeks including *Cats* and *Les Miserables* which were booked months in advance except for a third row seat for one in *Les Miserables* and a second row seat for one in *Cats*. Remember, seats for one are typically more available and generally better located than seats for two or more. If I had been two I couldn't have seen either play.

Unfortunately, in Mexico a woman alone is treated better if she speaks the language. Regrettably, men and couples are waited on first and accorded the choicest accommodations. But it's close, so you could take a week or two and see the main sights or if you have someone to travel with, you could RV it. Don't RV it alone. Southeast Asia is not only safer but there's little if any discrimination. Asian men are usually polite friends and guides and in Singapore, Taiwan and Hong Kong they're delighted to be with an American woman and pleased to show their country. They learn English and you get a personalized tour. Sometimes they'll arrive at your door with a friend in tow to demonstrate their honorable intentions. But don't get careless, there's good and bad in every culture.

Surprisingly Japan has few English-speakers and it appeared to me that women still walk three paces behind men, but you can teach English for $50 an hour, eat inexpensively at stand-up noodle shops or department store basements and stay in economy guest houses for an affordable trip. An ordinary room costs upwards of $200 and finding a decent place while cruising around in an expensive taxi isn't my idea of a good time. So if Japan is your country of choice call the Japan National Tourist Organization at 212-757-5640 and ask for the Welcome Inn Reservation Center budget hotel service. They'll arrange pensiones, hotels or traditional Japanese inns at fairly reasonable rates. It helps to know someone in Japan as women alone are suspect and/or disregarded.

Taiwan also has few English-speakers and while I wouldn't say this country's exceptional, if you've traveled extensively, it's noteworthy. I ate my first snake in Taiwan. It was delicious. And I'm not sure I'd want to guess what else I ate but everything was tasty, and high tea at the major hotels was a mouth-watering treat. Shopping for clothes and jewelry was fun but Taiwan gets cold in winter so I didn't stay long.

Most countries sincerely appreciate people learning even a little bit of their language. We can be so lazy sometimes. Just master "hello," "goodbye" and "thank you" on the plane or in your hostel. Ask for pronunciation at the front desk; they'll be genuinely pleased. The two countries that were not pleased when I attempted their language, nor were they anxious to help me learn, were Northern France and Southern Belgium which is also French speaking. All others seemed delighted. Remember that wherever you go you're somewhat of a U. S. Ambassador. You just might be the only Western woman some people will meet in a life time. Blow their negative conceptions of Americans by being one of the nicest and friendliest people they've met.

Egypt's dark secretive tombs and mysterious pyramids will transport you back to Biblical times with men wearing robes and headdress, riding camels and donkeys along the dusty palm lined roads. Expect to see Joseph and Mary around the next bend while the blistering sands of the Western Sahara burns indelibly into your soul.

A vague and distant sense of the Divine abounds, making one feel merged with the universe. And don't leave Cairo without exploring the spectacular museum. Be aloof with Egyptian men to avoid being touched or followed. If you want seclusion, slip on a chatower. Otherwise, try to visit during Ramadan . . . a religious holiday when men aren't supposed to think of sex. It's no guarantee, but it helps. And what's a chatower you ask? It's those black robes with slits to peer out of. You may have seen them on TV or in the movie *Not Without My Daughter* starring Sally Fields. It's not without reason that the women wear these robes if you've studied the Arab cultures or know anything about the Islamic religion.

Brazil is a visual paradise with long lovely beaches and lots to see but, as in a few parts of Africa, violent crime is rife and I don't recommend it without extreme precautions. However, should you visit this picturesque Portuguese speaking country, the food is delicious and exceptional leather products are available for a song at the flea market in Rio. There's much to see and do but watch your suitcase and fanny pack like a hawk and don't mail anything home as it probably won't arrive.

Lush tropical Sri Lanka lies off the Southern tip of India. Somerset Maugham-type hotels with fifteen foot high ceilings and antique furniture are available for $13 right on the beach outside of Colombo. The scenic train ride up the mountain through rice paddies, villages and jungles (definitely a Disney "E" ticket ride) transports you to the pinnacle village of Kandy. If Sri Lanka resolves her internal disputes, and constant begging doesn't bother you (don't even think of making eye contact), it's a captivating island to explore. However, the food, the coffee and even the rice tasted like mud to me. Indian food is so delectable, it puzzles me what could have happened to Sri Lanka. A good place to diet. On buses they put me in the front seat in the hopes that the bus wouldn't be bombed since it had a much needed tourist on board. I didn't mind since it was also in my best interest that we not be bombed.

Many women are flocking to the Eastern Bloc countries now that they're open, but even though these countries are poor, it can't be done on a shoestring unless you know someone. The shopping is depressing because there isn't much to buy but the people are wonderful. The food is basic and healthy and a trip here will make you glad to live in the United States if you aren't already.

I've touched only briefly on Europe because so many books on the subject already exist. So let me just briefly state that if you haven't been there, it's magnificent. Ride a bike, catch a train or rent a car but see it. Avoid Southern Italy and Spain if macho disturbs you and watch your belongings in Italy especially. Eurail passes must be purchased before going and they're pertinent to taking advantage of one of the most incredible aspects of Europe: dozens of countries with imposing vistas and sumptuous cuisine in a short space of time and distance. I love all of Europe and would recommend that at some point in your life you should see it. It's breathtaking. And just as an aside, leave each country as pristine and unspoiled as you find it no matter where you travel. Of course you already knew this but it's worth mentioning. Leave only footprints and goodwill.

Growth can be defined by pushing out boundaries and thinking beyond barriers and confines. The world is spectacular and the possibilities are limitless. It's all up to you. If a mid-aged, divorced, middle-income, mother of four like me can explore the world alone on a shoestring, why not you? I've met women in their eighties and young women in their teens all traveling alone. You can be self-limiting or self-expanding and only you can choose. Doing "nothing" is choosing limits. Doing "something" is enlarging your frame of reference and pushing beyond the fringe. If you think you can't, just S-T-R-E-T-C-H. The following chapters are how to begin.

Bamboo Huts & Train Whistles

““I think that to get under the surface and really appreciate the beauty of any country, one has to go there poor.”

-Grace Moore

If you purchase your accommodations simultaneously with your airline ticket it will cost double what you can acquire on your own not to mention that you're giving up your right to *choose.* If it doesn't unnerve you to buy a ticket without lodgings, it's unquestionably the most adventuresome and financially astute thing to do. Otherwise you're stuck with exceptionally vapid tourist hotels in dull tourist areas for additional capital, not to mention costly single supplements. In my early travels before I knew not to use travel agents, I purchased accommodations and even agreed on an "upgrade". Well of course the agent wanted to get the most out of me and I foolishly ended up in a boring new high rise hotel on a main street rather than a charming Tiki hut motel I would have chosen on my own. Pre-booking removes spontaneity and freedom of choice.

One pleasant way to locate unique accommodations is in conversation with fellow travelers and/or plane passengers who may be returning. An Australian publishing company entitled *Lonely Planet* is probably the best book for bargain housing to Asian countries, South America, and Africa. Check your local book store. If they don't have them they'll be happy to order them. They're just packed with thrifty lodgings. Buy one book which encompasses several countries so you're not loaded down with travel guides. Exchange books and novels you're finished with at used-book stores found in most large cities or with fellow travelers. It's especially interesting to find a book that has markings and comments from another traveler. And it might not seem kosher to tear a book apart but if you have a thick book and will only be using a small portion of it, rip out the part you need in order to limit weight and bulk. You can tape it back in when you return or give it to people headed for the area you just left. Sharing information is fun!

If you enjoy shopping, just consider accommodations another form of the same. As a rule of thumb, a good place to start looking for budget hotels in metropolitan areas is around bus or train stations, especially in Europe. Most stations have accommodation booths and bulletin boards but you can put your suitcase in a locker and just walk a couple of blocks around the station and usually you'll find something. In Asia, Australia, New Zealand, the Greek Islands and parts of Europe, people will be waiting at the train stations with pictures and little write-ups in English about their accommodations and they'll take you there themselves if you choose to go. Don't forget to bargain though, and also try to choose a location conveniently located so you can walk to town. And unless they're heavily booked, only reserve one day at a time so you can conveniently move if you like. One charming little Chinese hotel in Northern Malaysia had a noisy night club next door that rollicked till 3:00am. Not a happy night. When I complained at the front desk they gave me back ten cents (the room itself was only $7.00 which is about average for that part of Malaysia). But any refund hardly compensated for my lack of sleep even if it had been the full $7.00. And if I had paid for three or four nights I would just be out that money.

In Candidasa, Bali I found grass huts on the beach for $3 a night including a breakfast of mouth-watering black rice pudding with bananas and fresh coconut; a gigantic juicy fruit salad; or an American breakfast of sizzling bacon, eggs and toast . . . your choice and included in the price. Quaint huts such as this abound in Bali. In Thailand I slept on a futon in a bamboo cottage on the River Kwai for $4 a night contrasting with the elegant exotic hotel in Java for $10 with a shimmering pool, afternoon tea and snack and full-on breakfast of eggs, bacon and toast.

The average cost of my lodgings on my latest venture comprising beach huts, hotels, pensiones, trains, bamboo huts, YMCAs, YWCAs and B & B's but excluding stays in friends' homes, was $11 a night. And renting your home or apartment while away makes it even more affordable to travel overseas. Lively backpacker hotels in New Zealand and Australia, unique YWCA's in India, Greece, Hong Kong, Europe and anyplace I can find them, all afford a clean comfortable nights sleep. If you're invited to spend the night in someone's home and it feels safe, by all means do so. You could have an incredible cultural experience and gain lifelong friends. Being alone means you're absolutely sovereign. Stay wherever you like at any given moment. Even sleeping on an overnight train, as the rhythmic clacking of the wheels convey ever near the next intriguing port of adventure, feels exhilarating, bold and free.

Remember, economizing isn't really the issue but merely a somewhat interesting necessity to full exploration of a culture... a way to see more for less. Authentically experiencing a culture sharpens the senses and intensifies everything including life itself. To be a tourist is being wholly protected from novelty and contrast. Residing in the glass bubble of fine hotels and tour guides, you're consumed with the mechanics of travel rather than the sensations of the culture, the educational aspect inherent in displacement. Insulated against unknown but potentially rewarding experiences, against surprises, and mysteries you will lose the knowledge of your Self alone.

Planes, Trains & Boats

"Railway aids traveling by getting rid of all avoidable obstructions of the road, leaving nothing to be conquered but pure space."

-Ralph Waldo Emerson

Infinitely more can be seen and learned traveling overland than by flying, so check with the ticket agent, Global Assist, or discover on your own through books or friends how it is to travel by land. If the distances aren't too vast, it's safe, and you have the time, definitely do it. You might save on airfare but even if you don't, it's still imminently more rewarding to travel on land and see captivating exotic landscapes as opposed to flying over it and viewing the inside of a DC-10. The only place I couldn't travel overland safely as a single female alone was when I wanted to go from Kenya down to Johannesburg. I'm brave. I've traveled all around India, Turkey, and all the other countries I've written about in this book. I resented the man who sold me my tickets telling me I couldn't do that. I thought, "I'll show him!" But he was right. It isn't safe. If you want to go from Kenya to Johannesburg, fly.

Buses can be an interesting way to travel depending on the particular bus. Quality varies greatly relative to the country you're in.

If you're taking a long trip through Australia, Europe or New Zealand the buses have videos and large comfortable lounging chairs. It's quite a pleasant experience. Journeying from Brisbane to Cairns, Australia was terrific. Carefree happy travelers all (my bus companions and I), we watched four videos and saw expanses of shining red outback, hundreds of kangaroo, and striking countryside we would have missed on a plane. I flew back to Sydney because 18 hours on a bus is tiring, but the bus did save money and I'd do it again just for the adventure. The same thing applies with the reverse route from Jakarta through Java to Bali. I took the train to Yogyakarta from Jakarta and then rode to Bali on a bus I wouldn't have chosen. If you're traveling a lengthy distance, go directly to the bus station and purchase the ticket yourself rather than allowing a local to take you to some mystery vehicle the morning of your departure (as I foolishly did on that Java/Bali ride). I got stuck on a cheap local bus that stopped every 15 minutes to pick up mail, passengers, chickens, and produce. It was congested and dirty, everyone was smoking, there was no air conditioning and no one to talk with. On a short ride, this is local color. On a long ride the discomfort isn't worth the pennies saved. I saw enchanting sights along the way, but before purchasing a ticket, I should have inspected the bus. I learned the hard way. In most developing countries unless you purchase your ticket at the bus depot they'll tell you it's a first class bus when it's not, and air conditioning and comfortable seats can make the difference between joy and misery. That Java/Bali ride, except for the scenery, was ten hours of misery. Would I do it again? You bet. I'm not a glutton for punishment, but I am a traveler accepting the good and the bad as perfect aspects to an adventure. If I didn't want change I'd have stayed home.

In Turkey the buses average out to be about a dollar an hour and the longest trip I took was 12 hours.. At the bus depot you stand in front of the bus you'd like to take, the porter will load your suitcase onto the bus and take you to the desk where you purchase your ticket. The buses stop at wonderful eating places along their routes and everyone is friendly . Most men smoke and if it's cold outside and the windows are closed it's an adjustment. Most countries still allow smoking everywhere and if you're a non smoker you just have to overlook it. In Indonesia they smoke clove cigarettes which at least don't smell as bad but I understand are worse for your health. I'm not sure if that applies to second hand clove smoke, however. I do like the smell. I like the smell of the incense burning in a lot of stores throughout Asia, India, and Africa and even indulged in smoking a hooka pipe in tea houses in Egypt. They soak regular tobacco in treacle (a delicate sweet honey) for six months then they form a little ball with it and place it in the small bowl at the top of the pipe. The water cools the smoke so it doesn't burn your throat and the experience was relaxing and left me feeling a little drunk and singing Egyptian folk songs which don't even exist. It cost about a quarter to do this and I'm sure I did it more than I should have because after I left Egypt I missed it. In some of the interior Turkish villages the school children can be very excited to see an American on the buses and they love to have their pictures taken; they're so sweet. They gave me little trinkets so I went in a nearby store and bought them candy. They spoke little English and I couldn't speak their language but their faces, smiles and gestures spoke mountains. Being an Islamic country you'll see lots more men out and about than women as most Islamic women tend to stay home. A woman alone is a rare sight and this applies to Egypt as well, of course.

In developing countries, always take the highest class seat available on a bus or train because the difference is only a few dollars and the difference in comfort can be phenomenal. In most of Europe, the majority of trains and buses are excellent regardless of which class seat you select with the possible exceptions of Italy, Spain, and Portugal. The same is true for Australia and New Zealand... most buses and trains are great.

In Kenya the trains are hot, cramped, and bumpy while most safaris are superb but outrageously expensive. Kenya is the only place I was fearful for my safety while traveling overseas. Nairobi is nicknamed Nairobbery because of violent crime. It's unsafe to go out alone at night or to cross the park by oneself even during the day, but the wild animals in their natural habitat move and breathe with a grace and fluidity found only in the African jungle. Here you will see giraffe and elephant, hippo and tiger, baboon, wildebeast, and nearly every manner of wild animal. At Tree Tops Lodge I was transfixed watching the animals drink from the watering hole, when suddenly everything became very still and all of the animals turned to face one particular spot in the jungle. Shortly the answer appeared... a graceful sleek lion sauntered majestically into the clearing. Truly the King.

If you're flying to pristine Singapore, board a train headed for the verdant jungles and steamy tropical rain forests of Malaysia discussed in an earlier chapter. The merry click clack clicking of the tracks beneath the wheels lulls you ever near happy, smiling Thailand....a brilliant way to travel, incredibly inexpensive and clean. The porters make up the beds with crisp snowy sheets and the rhythmic pace invades one's psyche like lapping ocean waves, rocking its sojourner gently to sleep. My train ticket from Singapore through Malaysia into Northern Thailand was under $50. Meals are additional, delectable, and cost about $2.There are three main classes of trains in Asia: One is international (the optimum), the second is the express (not too bad), the third is rapid (definitely not), followed by quite a few below that (kill me first). Trust me when I say, travel international or express only.

Europe has its share of charming canals, meandering rivers, and serene reflective lakes, so boating is a brilliant way to tranquilly view the charming towns and countryside adorned with tiers of grape fields, majestic Gothic cathedrals, and magnificent castles. Kick off your shoes, lean back in the chair and sip Europe's best wines as life glides oh so gently by. Eurail passes allow travel on almost any train, some boats and ferries in nineteen European countries excepting England, North Africa and parts of Ireland. Two months on first class coach is under $900. Two weeks is less than $400 and all Eurail passes must be purchased before entering the continent. In England obtain a seven day bus pass for six pounds twenty pence at the train station or bus depot and jump on any bus or tube in London at any time. For the best view sit in the front seat on the top deck of a red double decker bus. A one day pass is two pounds thirty, so the seven day pass is the best buy and you'll need one of your photos for the ticket. Hopping on cable cars, trolleys or local busses is an exceptional way to see any large city for a pittance. Happy hours glide by on the trolleys in Vienna, Austria, Belgrade, Yugoslavia, Hong Kong, and Switzerland along with phenomenal scenery.

In India a special car is reserved for " women only" traveling on overnight trains. Meals are very good and you can order meat or vegetarian. I always eat vegetarian in India because it's safe and delicious. The train car for women is comfortable and discreet, but for safety's sake I recommend chaining your suitcase to the seat on all overnighters in all countries. Though I've never personally had anything stolen on a train, plane, or bus, it just pays to be safe.

Some women enjoy organized group tours with imposed schedules and companions. The obvious disadvantages are: winding up in some tiresome tourist spots and eating boring meals that have been planned for tourists. You're not as free to explore, possibly herded around like sheep and told when to smile and clap and eat. "Have your luggage outside your door by 3:00am." What a drag! It's extremely limiting. You'll be viewed in a separate light by the inhabitants of the area, if you even get to meet them; a different experience altogether. You'll pay more but most importantly, you'll miss out on the incredibly rewarding experience of traveling on your own and greeting the world.

In most countries it's possible to rent a car, but the expense of insurance, gasoline, parking, etc., may not be worth the trouble. Often you meet someone with a car who's going your way and you can chip in on petrol and ride with them. Or you can rent one and have someone chip in with you, but this can be a hassle. You're much freer using public transport or, if you're extremely adventuresome, in New Zealand, Australia, Tahiti, or parts of Europe, hitch-hike. In Third World countries transportation's so cheap, go first class or just have fun riding bikes and such. I love the rickshaw-type open air transportation and it's mere pennies... my favorite for short jaunts. See more up close and the rhythmic leisurely pace is wonderfully intoxicating. Now why are you thinking of the hooka pipe again just because I said the word "intoxicating". Stop that. It was just on that one trip, OK?

For brief excursions and great cultural color take local buses, rickshaws, mopeds, bikes, tuk tuks, bemos, ox carts, or what-have-you, depending on availability. Be prepared to share a seat with an animal, three people or a basket of fish (smelly local color). In Singapore taxis are inexpensive, the bus system is extremely efficient and the subway is actually beautiful! In Sydney, Australia quaint red buses charge only $5 a day to stop at all the local places of interest and you can get off and on at your leisure. Sydney's exquisite red tile roof tops and meandering parks and bay leave one breathless. Have your camera ready for a picture from the plane when you fly in.

In Cairo, Egypt one can luxuriate on a languorous boat ride down the Nile to the ancient, frozen-in-time capitol of Luxor. No, they don't have hooka pipes on the boats, will you stop? Rent a bike and ride the dusty roads through this sleepy, historic city for an intriguing education. As a matter of fact, if you're able to ride one, rent bikes wherever possible. They're inexpensive healthy exercise (as opposed to smoking hooka pipes!) and provide complete freedom. In Kathmandu, Nepal it's great fun to bike the rutted, winding dirt roads. Nepal's filth is softened by the vivid, multi-colored wares hanging in store fronts and magnificent snow capped Himalayas looming grandly in the background against the azure sky... although these majestic mountains were generally shrouded in clouds. Riding a bike here affords a close up inspection of these intriguing, exotic surroundings as well as leisurely viewing of the distant panoramic vistas and vibrant sunsets. A country for women with cast iron stomachs as the grime of the place creates daily health problems, and don't believe a word you hear from the locals. If you have a question, ask four or five people and then figure it out yourself. Hiking and camping gear can be rented very cheaply in Kathmandu if you're well enough and if you plan to hike the Himalayas you need to know about altitude sickness which affects one in four people. The sickness occurs because of oxygen depravation which begins between 6000 to 12000 feet above sea level with possible symptoms of a headache, nausea, insomnia, fatigue, shortness of breath and loss of appetite. If you take it real easy the first few days, drink plenty of liquids and don't consume alcohol you may be OK. In Kathmandu accommodations, food, local crafts and jewelry are all inexpensive, but bargain. It's part of the game.

Try to reconfirm plane reservations 48 hours before departure and if your flight is delayed causing you to miss a connecting one, get rebooked and your ticket validated by the airline that caused the delay. They may also provide you with a hotel if the delay is overnight but you may have to argue to get it . Start with a friendly optimistic attitude and go from there. A government publication, *Fly Rights: A Consumer Guide to Air Travel,* explains everything from over booking to lost luggage on American planes. You may have more rights than you know. Send $1.75 to Superintendent of Documents, Consumer Information Center, Dept. 133B, Pueblo, Colorado 81009. And if you're on a foreign airline it will all depend on the airline. I've had hysterically funny experiences on foreign airlines. One time I was on Egypt Air and had requested a nonsmoking seat. The men on each side of me proceeded to light up once the plane took off and I asked the flight attendant why they were smoking when these were non-smoking seats. He informed me that *my* seat, was, indeed, a non-smoking seat. Theirs were not. I stood up, looked at my seat, and, sure enough, it wasn't smoking!

No matter the mode of transportation, whether it's a donkey cart in Egypt, a tuk tuk in Thailand, a bemo bus in Bali, a rickshaw in Java, an elephant in Myanmar (Burma), a train, bamboo barge, boat, bus, or camel, the key word is: GO. Do it. Ride everything, go everywhere... S-T-R-E-T-C-H. Someone once said "Free men dragging their feet will be passed by slaves dragging their chains." Don't let that be you. Even if you have a chain, pick it up and dance.

Playing It Safe

"Who goes softly goes safely,
and he that goes safely goes far."
-(Italian)

Why are you traveling? Do you hunger to escape a ho-hum existence, long to explore other continents and cultures, desire to delve into your self and find you're more self reliant and adventure-some than you ever thought possible? Do you need to just leave home and hibernate for awhile? Or is your life perfect in most ways and you just love excitement, dreaming of being carried away to an exotic land? Do you like yourself well enough to occasionally need to be truly alone? Are you willing to take the chance to learn more about yourself than you ever knew before? Traveling solitary takes away the safety net of family, friends and familiar surroundings to put you on the exquisite precipice of life itself. The risks are few if you follow a few guidelines and safety precautions, and the rewards are countless.

Since you only have one piece of luggage (discussed in a later chapter), someone might ask you to check an extra suitcase through customs. Regardless of how innocent or pathetic they appear, don't do it. It could be drugs, contraband or *anything*. It might even be nothing but why risk it. If you ever have the slightest doubt about a safety factor, follow your instinct. Women have fantastically well developed intuition and if you think back, usually accurate. Learn to trust your intuition. The Eastern cultures place high value on the knowledge gained through intuition. Perhaps we need this lesson in our culture today. Always use your incredible intuition when traveling solo.

Be discriminating regarding attire. When you're by yourself, men may glance your way more and wonder why you're alone. They may even have the audacity to think you're alone because you want to be with *them.* More people travel in twos and, previously, more men traveled solo than women. In recent years however, the number of women traveling alone has more than doubled and while there may be lots more of us out there and, indeed, there may be some safety in that, inappropriate dressing courts disaster in many foreign ports.

It's advisable in many countries not to wear shorts or anything suggestive. If you want to adapt, wear the apparel of the country. If you do choose to wear shorts, wrap a sarong over them until you're in a suitable situation. Assimilate and for optimum safety try not to offend. In India I was treated more deferentially by the male population after donning a sari and adopting the local female populations' demeanor of aloofness. Of the countries I've been to, Western clothes and a friendly American attitude can mean availability in India, Greece, Egypt, Israel, Spain, Mexico, Italy, and most mid-Eastern and predominantly Muslim countries. Stepping off the plane in Singapore I was disconcerted in my serendipitous apparel consisting of flip flops, sarong and T-shirt; everyone was nicely dressed. It just all depends on the country. Southeast Asia is generally casual and wearing flip-flops, a wrap around skirt and t-shirt is normally OK . . refreshingly cool and comfortable.

In large part, how a woman is regarded is based on the religion of a particular country and tradition. The Hindu and Buddhist religions are found throughout Southeast Asia and India along with many others including Christianity. The Buddhist religion is non-violent, sometimes to the point of not even stepping on insects. Indonesia is principally Moslem but being racially mixed it's a very laid-back form of Islam compared to Arab countries. If you're in a strict Moslem country you'll know right away by the prayer chanting that's piped out over a loudspeaker from the mosques. You'll wake up to it at six in the morning and it reverberates off and on into the night.

It's my experience that many Moslem males hold women in disregard and I've had a few problems. However, it varies from man to man and I found the Malaysian and Turkish Moslems to be inoffensive. There's no hard and fast rule. The owner of the houseboat I stayed on in Kashmere, India was charming and kind. But if you haven't traveled extensively alone, avoiding hard core Moslem areas might be advisable with the exception of Malaysia and Turkey. Combined with the anti-American sentiment in some mid-Eastern countries, Western women need to be especially careful. Wear clothes that fully cover your arms and legs and most Islamic women cover their hair as well so I'll leave this one up to you. I only covered my hair on two occasions and that was because I was walking quite a long distance alone down a street congested with Arab males and another time just because I wanted to identify with the women in Turkey. In Turkey it isn't as if they have a choice to be a different religion. The Islamic religion is the country's religion and if you don't follow suit you can be killed. That's that. Moslem or die.

If you decide to drink alcohol in a foreign country, stay accessible to your hotel or at least eat enough to avoid becoming intoxicated. The heat and humidity in tropical climates can make you drunk before you know what hit you and when inebriated, you could be easy prey for complications. Alcohol is also dehydrating and in these hot countries you need all the fluid you can get. Carrying a water bottle on a strap is advisable and wear a hat to keep the blazing sun from giving you sun stroke.

Don't be under the very American impression you must be friendly to strangers. If someone approaches you or starts walking or talking with you and you're not interested or comfortable, cross the street, go in a store, or ask a policeman for assistance. Approach someone who's immediately available with whom you feel more secure, just for safety. On the whole, you will be absolutely safe. Just be cautious. Use your feminine intuition to pick up on a strangers' energy and vibrations.

Say "no" to guides who offer to take you to outlets or markets. They get a commission on whatever you spend so you pay more than if you went on your own and he may later expect a fee. In Morocco a "guide" said all the hotels were full and that the old part of town was dangerous so he would take us (I met a Canadian couple on the ferry to hang out with) to the new area where he was sure there were available rooms. He would stop the taxi and run into the hotel to supposedly check availability. All hotels seemed to be full. Well, guess what we discovered after about 45 minutes of this and a sizeable taxi fare? He was asking for a cut from each hotel for bringing us there. They would tell him "No" and he would take us to the next hotel. He also got a cut from the taxi driver ! We eventually ended up finding our own accommodations in a charming old hotel overlooking the harbor in the lovely older part of town he had said to avoid. Also, if something seems like a spectacular bargain, it's probably not. In Bombay, India, a boy was selling gorgeous saris for three dollars. On close examination and a little pull the material came apart in my hands. So be wary. That elephant hair bracelet in Kenya may be made of wire. Those Gucci watches in Bali are copies.

When making a reservation for the next country, be sure to consider arrival time. Leave a country as early in the morning as possible so you arrive at your next destination with enough time to leisurely locate comfortable accommodations. Try to arrive in each country during daylight hours... the earlier the better, for obvious reasons: walking around streets carrying a suitcase at midnight and knocking on closed doors isn't advisable.

When you are in the airport itself, be aware of a few tricks that can be played both at home and abroad: If you're standing in a phone booth or talking on a public phone and someone comes up and asks a question, he may be distracting you while another person grabs your suitcase which is probably on the ground next to you. Or someone can squirt catsup on your shirt or shoe, while another person will offer a cloth or handkerchief to wipe it off. During the distraction, the second person or even a third person, will abscond with your bag. The point is to distract you long enough for the theft to occur. Rarely is the person doing the distracting the one who actually takes your suitcase. Even security check points in airports can be targets for criminals: You place your bag on the conveyor, some-one steps in front of you with lots of coins and metal in his pockets, so he gets stopped and checked. In the meantime, someone in front of him has taken your bag.

To avoid becoming a victim of this type of crime, stay as much in contact with your bag as possible. For instance, when standing at a pay phone, place your bag firmly between your feet. When sitting, put your foot on your bag or place your leg over it. It's easy to dose off while waiting for a plane or train and that's when luggage can disappear. At the security gate, don't let anyone step in front of you.

Traveling on ones' own provides a sense of courage, intensity, and autonomy you may never have felt before. To know you're capable of exploring the world unaccompanied, greatly enhances self esteem... a crucial aspect of safety. Your attitude echoes through your body language. If you're relaxed, self-assured and friendly, it reflects back. If someone senses fear in you, you're more likely to have difficulties. In all of life, what you put mental energy on is what you will likely manifest for yourself. "Think positive and carry a big stick" might be a good quote in certain countries. On my first trip around the world in 1975, I took a karate class so I could defend myself. It wasn't needed but it assisted me in feeling more self assured. If it would relieve fear, take a self defense class before departing. Feeling safe and being safe are closely connected. If you're lost or nervous, walk tall and proud with your chin up. Stride confidently and think happy thoughts. This works even at home: slump down and lower your head. How do you feel? Now sit with your spine straight as if your head was suspended from an invisible golden thread attached to the ceiling. How do you feel?

Fear of the unknown is a number one fear. It's natural and will dissipate when you reach your destination. However, if being in a particular country feels uncomfortable, leave it. Allow yourself two to three days to be certain, and then move on. I'm not going to recommend dangerous countries though, so you'll be fine. Scared to visit Turkey after seeing the movie *Midnight Express,* I pressed on despite my fears and now I would return tomorrow if I had the time and money. It's the most historically significant country I've been to bar none, the people are friendly, the food's delicious and cheap. You might even discover that many if not most countries are safer than home. Sixty-one percent of women say they feel unsafe in their own neighborhoods. Someone once asked me where I experienced the most fear on my latest trip and I had to answer truthfully that it was on the freeway drive home from LAX to Long Beach.

It may be wonderfully romantic on a moonlit tropical island in the South Pacific to fall in love, but try to be circumspect with your emotions. When you come home, come home alone and consider who you've met, especially if someone wants to join you. Lots of people around the world would marry an American just to be in the U.S.A. . . especially in Third World countries. And if you're saying "No" to something, be sure your "No" is not taken for a "Yes." Be certain to give a concrete sign that you aren't available, if this is your intention. Smiling or speaking to men in some countries is considered a come-on. In numerous countries a smile is considered a non-verbal sign of welcome. Speaking to a man in Israel can mean you want to sleep with him! So be certain you know what you're feeling as well as what you're communicating.

Get a map of the city and mark your hotel location clearly. Ask one of the locals to write down the address in the native tongue so you can return easily. And before leaving your accommodation inquire how much transportation to your destination should cost. This will give you a guideline with the tuk tuk, taxi or bemo driver so you don't get ripped off. The more you know, the more confident you'll feel and the more bargaining power and power in general you'll have. If you do get ripped off it's not the end of the world; just consider that you learned something you didn't know before and don't do it again. When I arrived in New Zealand I had just been in Nepal, Turkey, Morocco, Portugal, India, and lots of countries I would consider less civilized than New Zealand. I was under the mistaken impression N.Z. was perhaps the safest country in the world. Imagine my surprise when my suitcase was stolen.

If you have a handicap or disability and require special attention, write: Travel Information Service, Moss Rehabilitation Hospital, 1200 West Tabor Road, Philadelphia, PA 19141 or phone (215) 456-9600. They have information to help you plan your trip abroad. I would love to write a travel book for women with disabilities or special needs but as of yet I haven't had the time or opportunity. But the psychological aspects mentioned previously would apply. I just have no knowledge of safety factors relating to this issue or how men in various countries would react, since men are generally the ones we speak of in relation to being safe.

Staying Well

"The country, your companions and the length of your journey will afford a hundred compensations for your toil."

-Orm, Remediorum Amoire 1.242

"If you have a somewhat sedentary lifestyle, start taking short walks each day before you leave, minutes to begin with, increasing to half an hour or an hour. Most likely you'll be doing a great deal of walking on your trip even if you use all the local transport mentioned previously. So beginning slowly and working your way up will prevent shin splints and sore muscles.

If you tend to have motion sickness, eat some ginger before you take a boat or plane trip. Ginger has been used in China for more than 2,500 years and also works well against heartburn. Fresh sliced ginger is best of course, but ginger ale, though not as powerful, is a handy substitute...anything ginger. Mix a half teaspoon of powdered or fresh ginger in tea or sprinkle powdered ginger on your food. This should alleviate any queasiness or heartburn. Dramamine is only a little less effective but can cause drowsiness.

Very few immunizations are required by law these days. Yellow fever is required in parts of equatorial Africa and Latin America, cholera in a few countries if you're entering from an infected zone and other immunizations aren't required but may be recommended for your own safety and protection. DPT, diphtheria and tetanus are recommended once every ten years. If you haven't had one recently, you might want to update. If you're traveling to undeveloped countries make sure you have a current polio vaccination and allow plenty of time as some vaccinations require eight to ten weeks before you can travel. A permanent hepatitis B vaccine just came out last year and I recommend getting one. A flu shot isn't a bad idea and they recently developed a life time pneumonia vaccination which, though not needed for travel, isn't a bad idea all the same. Consult your personal physician if you like or if you have a health plan use that, but get your shots. If you're traveling on a shoestring and you don't have health insurance, use your local city health department. There's a nominal charge and they'll record your shots in a health certificate to be carried in your fanny pack with your passport.

Upon venturing into a malarial zone bring the best mosquito repellent available; it's invaluable. If there's no one to put it on your back, lay your shirt on the bed and cover the back of it with repellent. Mosquitoes are more active in late afternoon or evening so replenish repellent more frequently at these times. Chances are slim that you would contract malaria but why chance it, and even normal mosquitoes are annoying pesky things. Avon has a great repellant/ sun screen/ moisturizer combination lotion that even smells good! Malaria pills can cause queasiness and they only protect against three types of malaria. There's about thirteen different kinds. I'm not saying you shouldn't take malaria pills; it's a terrible illness and one that comes back throughout a lifetime if contracted and can even be deadly. A series of pills to alleviate Malaria is available over the counter in many Third World countries and I carry these in my fanny pack. Most regions supply mosquito coils. These are similar to incense and repel mosquitoes in your cabin for approximately 8 hours at a cost of ten cents. It's expedient to light one before retiring. A fan in the room makes it impossible for mosquitoes to fly. Mosquito netting is also a deterrent and taking Vitamin B and/or garlic is said to repel them as well. Remember to avoid anything highly fragranced in mosquito infested areas as most perfume attracts them. Notice the percentage of DEET in mosquito repellent. The highest percentage of both DEET and metaisomer that I've found is in Moskal and the longer lasting, newer Ultrathon. These can be purchased in sporting goods stores or pharmacies. Estee Lauder has recently developed a sun screen that repels insects including mosquitos, but for convenience and utility, I carry Avon's Skin-So-Soft moisturizing sun care with citronella which, by the way, repels fleas and deer ticks as well and has a #15 SPF.

Traveling in developing countries, if you intend to be out in the wilds, it's advisable to carry purifying water tablets which can be purchased in sporting goods stores and pharmacies. Even brushing teeth or eating fruits and vegetables can make you ill if you're using contaminated water. Carrying a plastic bottle of water is wise... even in America. And always make sure the cap is sealed before buying water or you could get a bottle that's been used and refilled. A new portable purification system called Oasis looks like a regular water bottle but has a built-in three stage filter system and only weighs half a pound, costs $30 and not only purifies but makes water taste good too. A bit extravagant unless you travel a lot in out-bound areas where bottled water isn't readily available. If you haven't traveled before, developing countries may not be the best way to begin unless you love adventure and can laugh at predicaments. But if you can't laugh at life perhaps you should stay home with locked doors and if you weren't adventuresome you'd probably be reading a juicy novel now instead of this travel book. So on to the unpleasant stuff.

Sooner or later half of all travelers who go abroad get diarrhea. No big deal. You can take Pepto Bismol if you like or buy Imodium if it's really bothersome. The best natural remedy is bananas as they contain fluid-binding fiber with lots of potassium which is lost from diarrhea and perspiring. Potatoes contain twice the potassium of bananas but without the fluid-binding fiber (good if you're merely perspiring). Sometimes it's best to let nature take its course; there's something in your system that wants out and it may be better to let it go and drink lots of tepid tea and apple juice... the best fluid replacement for diarrhea because it's also rich in potassium and rebalances your electrolytes which get off balance with fluid loss. Low potassium or imbalanced electrolytes can cause weakness, dizziness or depression, so devour those bananas and sip that apple juice. If you're in the USA where power booster drinks for runners are available, drink them. Gatorade is now available in many countries and these same symptoms and remedies apply to sun stroke. Be sure to wear a hat in countries with unforgiving sun. Sun stroke can actually kill you. And don't forget to pour salt on your toothbrush to kill any bacteria that may be lurking there. Otherwise you'll re-infect yourself every time you brush.

A high concentration of garlic can get rid of parasites and worms both in humans and pets. It's one of the best medicinal plants there is and seems to work against viruses and yeasts as well. It's effective against nine antibiotic-resistant bacteria as well as having excellent cardiovascular benefits. So if you have persistent diarrhea or have perspired a lot, eat bananas, garlic, potatoes, rice, tea and apple juice. If you need something stronger, most medicines are available over the counter without a prescription in developing countries. Ask the pharmacist. If you do happen to pick up any type of organism at all, thoroughly clean your tooth brush after each brushing with a heavy salt solution or alcohol to kill the germs. Often we reinfect ourselves with colds, flu, and diarrhea by brushing with a bacteria filled toothbrush. And regarding teeth, a visit to your dentist might be prudent if your trip is lengthy. If you do get a tooth ache overseas, buy oil of cloves at a pharmacy to numb pain.

If you need medical assistance, your Embassy can advise you of doctors or emergency medical facilities. American embassies are there for us and American Express offices also offer this service along with 24 hour emergency numbers for doctors, hospitals, pharmacies and a legal hot line if you're carrying their card or checks.. In addition, American Express will make an appointment with the doctor for you. They'll recommend physicians and set up anything you need including covering medical expenses if you don't have the money (provided you have their card)... a nice service to know is there even if you don't use it. It might be more tedious through the American Embassy as American Express is a business specifically for travelers. If you do need the embassy, American Express will furnish their number and address as well. If you have any special medical needs you might want to become a member of the nonprofit International Association for Medical Assistance to Travelers (IAMAT, 716-754-4883). You'll receive a directory of certified English-speaking doctors as well as other health care providers.

If you take any prescription drugs, leave them in their original containers to avoid any trouble going through customs, and if it's serious, carry it in your fanny pack. Bring a letter from your physician if it's questionable and/or a written prescription. Antihistamines are good for any unexpected allergic reactions and can also double as a mild sleeping pill to help with jet lag. If you become sick after returning home from a trip, whatever your symptoms might be, be sure to tell your doctor where you've been.

Maintaining good health is of paramount importance on any trip and to do this easily, I recommend eating vegetarian whenever possible. If you feel you need more protein, fish is generally quite good, especially fish that swim as opposed to shell fish. Beef is probably more questionable but I've eaten delicious water buffalo steaks in Thailand that I couldn't differentiate from filets at home with no ill side effects. But to be certain, dine on fruit, carbohydrates and vegetables. In Sri Lanka I saw a side of beef hanging from a tree outside a restaurant and it had lots of flies on it. Who would eat there? Quite a few countries hang their beef out and now that I've ruined your appetite, let me just add that India's predominantly vegetarian, so delicious, healthy fare is plentiful. One of the least expensive meals I ate on any of my travels was a savory vegetarian meal somewhere in the heart of India. It was at an outdoor cafe, freshly prepared and delicious and cost two cents. I'll never forget it. And because India doesn't kill her cows, milk products such as yogurt and creamy ice cream are plentiful. The Indians also use herbs and spices in their cooking which aid in digestion and staying well.

Jet lag means your body rhythms are out of sync with the new time zone and you may have difficulty sleeping. You might feel tired during the day with a sense of exhaustion or disorientation. You may not be as hungry as you normally are and could have trouble concentrating or some memory loss. There's a variety of things you can feel from jet lag. A useful remedy is vitamins, especially amino acids. Begin taking them a month before departure and continue for a week after. But Melatonin is the very best remedy for jet lag by far, available in health food stores, it will relax you to sleep while boosting your immune system. I'm not against the use of caffeine to help in adjusting to a new time zone as well. Try to sleep on the flight if you can. Sleeping earlier on the flight will make you feel better than sleeping toward the end as landing effects pressure on the ears. Don't drink any caffeinated or alcoholic beverages on the flight. They're dehydrating. Acute low back pain is the second most common reason Americans see a doctor, with colds being first. If you have a bag or something to rest your feet on in the plane, this elevates your knees above your hips, taking the pressure off the back of your legs and putting the pelvis in a position that keeps the lumbar spine curving the way it should. Doing this will also prevent swollen ankles and feet. Before I started doing this, my feet would swell nearly a half size on long flights making it uncomfortable to walk around once I landed. And be sure to ask for a blanket and pillow when you first board. Placing the pillow between the seat and your lower back will counteract the tendency to slump which squeezes the ends of the vertebral disks, putting stress on them and cutting off necessary fluid. And once in flight some planes get very cold, so wrap up in your blanket. Get out of your seat and move around as much as possible. Stretch, and don't keep looking at your watch to see what time it is back home. The quicker you adjust to the new time zone the more energetic you'll feel.

Perhaps due to a guilty conscience over the way he treated his wives, King Henry VIII suffered from severe insomnia. His remedy was to stuff his pillow with hops. If you don't have hops or Melatonin, another natural sleep inducer is complex carbohydrates which have a calming quality... so eat a potato, some cereal or rice before bedtime and sleep like a baby. Go easy on the butter though as it counteracts the effect. Calcium is relaxing too; so I take a calcium pill just before bed time whether I'm traveling or not. After menopause women lose bone density so extra calcium slows this process down. Are you sensitive to noise? Soft-wax earplugs are surprisingly comfortable and can be found in most United States pharmacies. Pleasant dreams.

Obey your body. If it's lunchtime but you only want iced tea, have iced tea. If you're between meals but you feel the urge to eat, by all means do so. The two key words are: relax and enjoy. If you're weary, sit down and rest. Your body knows best what its' needs are. Observe attentively and follow that advice; you'll feel healthier in the long run. If you suffer from earache take an antihistamine one half hour prior to departure and chew gum while in flight. Be careful about chewing too much sugarless gum however as it contains sorbitol which can cause gas pains! Not a nice thing to experience on a long flight, or even a short flight for that matter...especially for those around you.

One fundamental key to a successful trip lies in finding humor in all things. Laugh and enjoy yourself. As in all of life, situations will arise that could upset you or you could choose to laugh. The choice is yours. You'll appreciate your trip much more if you're friendly, chuckling and going with the flow. The more you laugh the more liberated you'll be and that goes for all of life as well. I was on a sixteen hour bus trip squashed into a tiny seat next to a fossilized little old man who attempted to touch my left breast every time I fell asleep. Trying to maintain my sense of humor I now laugh at the situation which seems even funnier in retrospect. At the time, I suppose I was considering knocking out his last three teeth. The Thais have an expression which means "no big deal": "Mai pen lai" (pronounced my pen lie) and the Australians say "No worries, mate." That about sums it up. Mai pen lai, my friend.

Let's Eat

"Down to Gehenna or up to the Throne he travels the fastest who travels alone."

-Rudyard Kipling

If food is a major concern (and when is it not?) here's the scoop: Southeast Asia and India tend toward hot and spicy which aids in digestion, assists in alleviating colds and flu and raises metabolism. New Zealand, Australia, England and a few parts of Europe and Africa tend toward mild or bland. In most of Asia the food is incredibly mouth watering but don't eat the little red peppers unless you want to clean out your sinuses for a month (just kidding). If you do accidentally eat one, eat rice immediately to stop the burning. Drinking water won't dilute the sensation and may more widely distribute it. Food is tasty in Nepal but getting sick is practically inevitable. Whether it's from the dust that the women sweep into the air each morning or the oil and water used in cooking, eat lots of garlic and ginger for protection. As you probably know, Europe has varied and delicious food and safe water but it's more expensive than South East Asia and many Third World countries.

A good rule of thumb for inexpensive dining: look at the restaurant or food stall and its proprietor. If it and they look clean and healthy, chances are the food will be too. Look at fingernails and if they're dirty or there's a fly in the food case, forget it. In general, there are two main things to watch: water and fresh, uncooked food. Make sure the water is purified or boiled; and it's to no avail avoiding the water if you eat fruit or vegetables that have been washed with it. Ice can be a danger but most nice restaurants realize tourists will get sick if they fail to serve purified water and food and no one will come back for a second helping of touristas. If something tastes, smells, or looks a little off, don't eat it or *you* may be off.

In a few countries, despite your best efforts, you may have trouble. If you can check out the kitchen, do so. In a popular restaurant in Nepal, I observed an employee washing and drying dishes with a filthy rag I wouldn't use on my car tires, but I eat at food stalls throughout Thailand and Malaysia with no problem. Fresh fruit is in abundance and wonderfully juicy and exotic. So enjoy it but be careful not to consume too much in the beginning or you could end up with a tummy ache. First timers to New Zealand think they have diarrhea but its just too much kiwi. Kiwi in particular but fruit in general except bananas, tends to be laxative. However, kiwi is higher in vitamin C than oranges . . . great if you have a cold, and delicious. Or have you ever tasted rambutans, salaks or, my personal favorite, mangosteens? Yumm.

In Southeast Asia and more tropical climates you'll likely be eating rice and fruit frequently, possibly a much lighter diet than you're used to in America. You'll probably be walking and exercising more than usual too unless you jog or exercise a lot now. So your weight will probably balance itself out . . . if you're heavy you'll lose; if you're thin you may gain muscle.

More and more women are eating alone these days. Probably because it costs just about as much to buy food and prepare it at home and more of us are just too busy to cook. My favorite thing to make is reservations. But when you're traveling alone you don't have much choice one way or the other unless you're staying at an economy hotel with kitchen facilities. Eating alone isn't as bad as it sounds. As a matter of fact, if you're weight conscious, it's the wise thing to do. John and Elizabeth DeCastro, Professors of Psychology at

Georgia State University did a study that shows people who eat alone consume 403 calories during a meal. With one other person it jumps to 547. If you have four people eating together it leaps up to 664 calories each. And when six or more people are present it goes all the way up to 765. So it seems we're eating a great deal more with other people. The average amount consumed when you're alone is 47% carbohydrates, 37% fat and 16% proteins. But when you're with other people it's 42% carbohydrates, 40% fats and 18% proteins. So from this study it appears to be much healthier to eat alone. If you're overweight, traveling in Southeast Asia is probably the best weight loss program you'll ever come across in your life . . . especially if you forget to use bottled water to rinse your toothbrush. Just joking. Don't do it. Always rinse your toothbrush with bottled water in Third World countries. And if you're feeling sick, rinse it out with mouth wash or soak it in a heavy salt solution. We often reinfect ourselves daily with a bacteria filled toothbrush!

Most large hotels serve afternoon tea for about $5 which includes delicious sandwiches, exotic munchies, tea, coffee and scrumptious deserts. When I get tired of the bamboo huts and grass shacks, it's fun to spend a couple of hours luxuriating in air conditioned elegance with exquisite food in front of me. What an excellent way to pamper yourself. I do this at least once in almost every country. It takes the edge off economizing and in Japan, the basements of major department stores offer sizable free food samples and cheaper prices than restaurants. In Tokyo I eat at stand-up noodle shops and buy hot coffee in cans at vending machines for $1.50. Don't turn up your nose. I'm a coffee connoisseur too and this stuff is really quite good; almost as good as the $5.00 a cup coffee in Japanese restaurants.

If you don't enjoy airplane food, order vegetarian or seafood meals when you reconfirm your flight out of each country. I find their beef can be tough and overcooked, their chicken chewy. Austrian Air had the best meal and the most elegantly served food of any airline I've flown and it was on a short leg of an around-the-world flight underwritten by TWA. Kosher meals are also available on most airlines. But generally I've found plane food unappealing and merely a way to kill a little time on the flight. Sometimes the quality of food can be the country you're flying out of as much as the airline itself. Do you think airline food is filled with preservatives and fillers? Me too. But Delta Airlines has developed a healthy, delicious, non-alcoholic drink called Pawberry Punch . . . and American Airlines uses lemon juice and no preservatives on fruit and vegetables. "Heart healthy" meals can be pre-booked. So many airlines are picking up on the fact that people want healthy food when they fly. With the unhealthy aspect of being in a pressurized cabin for hours, who needs bad food as well. Three cheers for those airlines showing concern for our health.

Perhaps the ultimate in exotic dining abroad occurs when you've been invited to someone's home or get taken to a local neighborhood restaurant. It's impolite to refuse the local fare so if you're squeamish, don't ask what something is. If you tell them you're vegetarian ahead of time, you'll be fairly safe. After domestic violence, heart attack is the number two killer of American women today. We should focus on prevention by cutting dietary fat and cholesterol, not smoking, exercising regularly and maintaining a healthy weight. Walking is a great way to condition your heart and lungs but don't push too hard too soon. Reduce your pace if you can't speak easily in a conversational tone. Ultimately you should be healthier, more in control and confident after this trip. It all goes hand in hand. If you're healthier, chances are increased that you'll be happier. If you're happier and feel more confident your life should be more joyful. Feeling inner joy will make people want to be with you. Don't you enjoy being with happy people more than depressed ones? Well foreigners are no different. They aren't likely to invite you to their home if you look depressed. And don't be shy about asking locals where a good restaurant is. Not only do they know, many times they'll take you there or even ask to join you. If they don't speak English, use sign language to look like you're eating. They'll understand. Most restaurants that cater to travelers have English menus. If they don't hand you one in English, ask. It might have just slipped their mind or maybe it isn't apparent you're American.

Things Mother Didn't Tell You

"Of journeying the benefits are many: the freshness it bringeth to the heart, the seeing and hearing of marvelous things, the delight of beholding new cities, the meeting of unknown friends, the learning of high manners."

-Sadi

Make an attempt to learn the customs of various countries you'll be visiting. Americans don't have a reputation for being soft spoken or gentile and we're often presumptuous, expecting everyone to speak English and follow our protocol. So if you want to reduce the risk of an embarrassing *faux pas*, a little 94 page guide of American and foreign customs is published by the National Institute of Business Management entitled *Mastering Business Etiquette and Protocol* for $14.95 or see if your local library has it. If you intend to do business while you're traveling, I would recommend getting it. Otherwise, just plain logic and a friendly attitude will take you far. In numerous foreign countries, service in stores and restaurants is slower than we're used to and in many hot Latin countries shops close for afternoon siestas. In England, France and others, restaurants open late and then only serve during certain hours, so try to be patient. Part of the fun of travel is that things are different. Relax and adjust to these differences. Get on a slower pace; it's healthy.

In India try not to touch food with your left hand and always hand items to people with your right hand. The left hand is considered unclean. In Southeast Asia, touching children on the head is considered demeaning and their spirit gets taken away in the touch. Several countries feel the same about picture taking. In Bali and Mexico, it's against their religion to be topless on the beach. In Mexico you can even be arrested for being topless in a public place. In Bali they tolerate it but it doesn't endear us to them to break their religious customs. In Thailand, it's impolite to point your foot toward someone and a gross insult to show the bottom of your foot. Making a circle with your thumb and forefinger signifies "OK" and "right on," in the U.S.A., "money" in Japan, "zero" in France and is an obscene gesture in Brazil. Being tolerant is more than good manners . . . it's practical. An American became angry in a Thai restaurant, threw money on the floor and stomped on it. Thai money has a picture of their highly revered King on it so the American was thrown in jail. This was an unusual case, but it makes a point. Customs are the beliefs and values and as significant to them as ours are to us.

Show respect to leaders and consideration for religious beliefs. We're all people of this Earth and the country you're in is theirs, so be polite and deferential. Mind your voice (Americans are often loud) and your attitude. I was on a first class train traveling through the beautiful countryside of Germany and everyone was speaking softly and politely, everyone, that is, except an American woman who was speaking to her child and thought it was so cute she wanted everyone to notice, so her voice boomed throughout the whole compartment. I was embarrassed she was an American. Customs don't necessarily have anything to do with safety but they inevitably have a great deal to do with the impression we impart throughout the world.

Exemplify sincerity, friendship, and joy. We're accustomed to so much abundance and freedom in the United States, so when traveling, try to be good-natured and gracious. Most people consider the United States incredibly luxurious and many people want to come here for the incredible freedom and wealth. So before deriding our homeland, think how unappreciative and spoiled you'll appear. Just think of my Hungarian friend Hajnel who left all she had for freedom. And learn to slow down for Pete's sake. It isn't the end of the world if you don't make it to the Taj Mahal before 2:00pm, is it? You won't starve if lunch isn't on the table in fifteen minutes, will you? And where are you going in such a rush anyway? Relax. Soften. Unclench. Unwind. Take a deep breath and s-t-r-e-t-c-h.

When walking in foreign territory whether here or overseas, it will help ensure your safety if you don't appear uncomfortable... even if you are. Carry yourself with an air of certainty and confidence that conveys self assurance. Do your map reading in a restaurant or in your room and jot down directions on a piece of paper so you don't have to pull out the map on the street. In some countries such as Italy or Brazil, studying a map on the street is like holding up a sign that says rob me. But if someone looks civilized don't be afraid to visit with them. They may be travelers like yourself with creative ideas about where to stay, places to eat, or activities in which to indulge. You might manage, as I did when I went to Tokyo, to share a room with someone you meet on the plane. Tokyo's expensive so we cut costs and drank in information about each other's home lands. Last time I was in Switzerland she was getting married so I had the privilege of attending a lovely ceremony held in a quaint stone Church on a flower-strewn hillside.

An important time and money saver, if you have an American Express card, is to bring blank checks or your bank account number with you. If you need money, American Express will issue cash right on the spot. Once I was delayed 2 weeks in Hong Kong, waiting for cash to be wired from the States, and it cost over $150 to wire $1,500 not to mention valuable time lost. When cashing travelers checks always check the commission charged. Some places charge for the number of notes you change and some charge according to how much total cash you need. The American Express office doesn't charge and usually has a fair rate, but be prepared to wait in line.

Many countries have a black market. If on a hundred dollars the black market rate is not more than ten dollars per hundred I don't recommend it, and never change with someone off the street. Change with someone who has a business or home because you can easily be defrauded. Someone can perform slight of hand or simply rob you as happened to a friend of mine in Hungary. Be cautious if the rate they offer seems too good to be true; it's probably a setup. In Romania the legal rate was 11 to 1 and the black market rate was 100 to 1. Guess which I chose. But I knew people and knew there was no danger. In

Nepal I exchanged money in shops but I also exchanged at the bank because they ask to see your bank exchange slips when you fly out. Always save your bank exchange slips until you're out of a country. You may be asked to show them. When I was attempting to leave Romania they said I didn't have enough bank slips which of course I didn't, so I bribed them with a carton of cigarettes and a little American money and they were most happy. Otherwise I might have found myself in a kettle of fish so to speak. You may consider black market money unethical. If so, don't do it. I don't do anything that I would disrespect myself for. And when governments start being fair with their people, I'll be fair with them. Did you know that three quarters of our U.S. currency is overseas? Maybe my daughters have been shopping too much. Someone grab that Discover card! Just kidding. What we really need to do is ration politicians! That would solve the national debt right there.

If you have an ATM card ask your bank if it's available in countries you're visiting and if there's a charge for overseas use. You could benefit from the wholesale exchange rate as much as 7% over bank rates. And some countries won't buy their money back when you leave so don't cash more than you'll need. Each time you make a change from one monetary system to another it's going to cost, so again, don't cash too much. And don't accept very old or torn money as it might not be accepted in stores. Dollars are very popular in all countries and the larger the denomination the higher the exchange rate, but carrying large bills of cash can be risky so use your own good judgment. Do take thirty single $1 bills for tips and miscellaneous. Coins can't be cashed from one country to the next so spend them or give them as souvenirs upon returning home.

Place calls to home from overseas post offices or phone companies. Check to see if it's cheaper to call direct, collect, or via credit card. Never call from hotels unless price is no object. And certain times of day have better rates . . . just like home. And a secret most travelers don't know is that calling from abroad can be cheaper using a local phone card instead of an American based long distance service...but this only applies in countries that have the cards of course. They're pretty little collector items too. I still have mine from New Zealand.

Some countries such as Tahiti, Singapore and The People's Republic frown on tipping and in others such as England and New Zealand, tips are included in your bill. Check out the tipping system by asking another traveler or someone dining at the same restaurant. Never be afraid to ask questions; it could instigate a happy conversation or even a lifelong friendship.

In the East, custom dictates that you remove your shoes before entering Muslim mosques, Buddhist temples and Japanese homes and restaurants. Always place shoes neatly together facing the door you entered. In India and Indonesia, follow the lead of your hostess.

Women must not touch or hand anything to a Buddhist priest. If you do, you'll offend not just him but everyone around you. Now why doesn't this apply to men? Is there something I don't know? I'd sort of like to touch one just to see if he'd disappear or explode or go up in a puff of smoke. And don't call anyone by her first name unless invited to do so. And don't go in temples if you're on your period. WHAT? Just thought I'd throw that in to see if you're paying attention. Who the heck's gonna know? If you don't tell them, I promise I won't.

A shared cup of coffee, tea, or a soft drink often precedes business dealings... even shopping. In Turkey I was offered tea about 20 or so times a day. ("Where is the toilet?" is a good thing to learn in all languages.)The tea is a delicious hot lemony mixture but I obviously had to draw the line on how much I could consume. I think they feel if you drink and chat you'll feel obligated to buy so try to drink where there's something you would, indeed, like to purchase. And in Thailand and most of Southeast Asia it's believed a prosperous day will ensue if they make a sale to the first customer entering their shop and a bad day if they don't. So if you know what you'd like to purchase, go early for the best bargaining. Wouldn't it be great if Nordstroms would adopt that policy?

If an Arab man finds you attractive he'll pull his beard. An Italian will place a finger on his cheek and turn it. A Greek will stroke his cheek and a Frenchman will kiss his fingertips. A Brazilian will put an imaginary telescope to his eye. So slather some mud on your face, girls. (Just kidding). And I have no idea what a woman in these countries would do if she found you attractive. In Thailand she'd probably approach you but when I was in Romania, being gay was a criminal offence with a long jail sentence. But don't be offended or nervous if you see men making the above gestures; it's actually considered a compliment. In Bulgaria and Greece shaking your head "yes" means "no." In the Middle and Far East, pointing with the index finger is impolite. Use your open hand instead. Any gesture that shows the other person the back of your hand is considered insulting.

Writing instruments such as Parker pens make excellent gifts to give a host anywhere around the world and in Southeast Asia people under 30 like T-shirts from any other country, especially from universities.

To aid with communication overseas, try these simple suggestions: 1) Enunciate clearly and slowly with pauses in between sentences, 2) Concentrate on one thought at a time, 3) Use hand gestures and visual aids. If you ask "do you understand?" you'll get a "Yes" even if they don't, so avoid questions with "yes" and "no" answers. If there's a misunderstanding, take the blame. If you ask directions in Southeast Asia, if the person you ask doesn't know he may feel humiliated so he'll tell you anything and you could end up in Tim Buck Two. Ask two people to be certain.

If you're confused as to which countries you'd most like to visit, look at the list you made and check out a video of that region from your local public library or video store. Some libraries even have foreign language tapes available. And someday maybe we'll have a video for women traveling alone. Maybe *you* will make one after the travel bug has gotten hold of you and you see how fun traveling the world solo can be.

Getting Out The Suitcase

"He travels safest in the dark night who travels lightest."

-Hernando Cortez

Being female myself I realize how you probably pack. Forget it. We're going to do it differently this time. Merely lay everything out that you just can't live without on this trip. Stop reading and go do it. Hey! Why are you still reading? I'll wait, I promise. Put the book down and go. OK. Done? Nah. You're still reading, but that's OK. We'll *pretend* you did it. Now divide it in half. Why are you laughing? I'm serious. Come on, just give it a try. Divide it in half. And this is really going to blow you away: of the remainder, relinquish half of that as well. Oh come on. You can do it. I have faith in you. You really didn't need those fake alligator boxer shorts anyway, did you? And now we're finally down to an amount you can easily carry because we're only taking carry-on luggage. I'm not joking. One small carry-on suitcase is all you really need. Don't stop reading. I've gone around the world three times on six month trips and this is all I took and all I needed. I'm going to give you a very specific list, so just relax, take a deep breath and repeat after me "I can do this. This is all I need."

Honestly, you'll feel liberated and most grateful during your actual trip. It may even surprise you how much fits into one tiny bag and how little you can actually get by on. Remember the last trip you took? How much of what you hauled with you did you actually use? Be honest. If you pack wisely you'll have all you need and then some. Trust me. Have I ever lied to you before? And you probably aren't planning a six month trip anyway, are you? How long are you going for? A month? Three weeks? Then I know you can do it. Follow my instructions, pack only what's listed on your check list and you'll have enough for six months. Honest.

You're infinitely freer if you take a suitcase you can easily handle yourself. And carry-on is imperative and ingenious if you're touring more than one country; luggage is inconvenient and cumbersome with precious time spent waiting for it to arrive at baggage- claim. You're not interviewing for the Miss America title so be a Traveler... pack lightly. And did you ever have lost luggage? What a headache. With carry-on you have it at your fingertips, thus, when you leave the airport you're the first one out the door (and the first one in the shops). They usually wave you right through customs too. Yeah! Freedom!

Purchase a carry-on size suitcase with large rubber built-in wheels. The best one I've found is by Delsey (Phone 1-800-558-3344 for availability in your area) but there are lots of others out there so check them all out and be sure yours has large rubber wheels. No, plastic is not OK. Read my lips: r-u-b-b-e-r. It costs about $130, has zippered outer pockets on both sides with a roomy inside compartment, is soft-sided which makes it expandable and the large sturdy wheels bounce easily over cobblestone and dirt streets. It's guaranteed for five years. Samsonite has a hard-sided carry-on with fairly decent sized wheels and a large pull-out handle for easy towing. When you're shopping, look at all of them but avoid hard little plastic wheels, a back pack or anything without a shoulder strap. When carrying or pulling, switch sides often to avoid straining your back and when lifting, keep your back straight, standing with the suitcase close by your side, bend both knees, grasp the handle and slowly straighten your knees. Most carry-on luggage has a pull-out handle these days. This handy dandy handle will prevent a sore back and muscle strain. Stand up straight as much as possible and on the plane, if you can store your suitcase under the seat it makes a great foot stool. If you have a bad back, this prevents having to lift it into the overhead compartment as well. My latest adventure began with eight pounds, ending with twenty-six so at various times I was carrying twenty-two to twenty-six pounds, which is fairly heavy. The sizable wheels and expandable sides were invaluable, but for comforts sake try to keep the weight at about 13 pounds if you can. Mail some items home when it gets too heavy. Wheels are indispensable, even if you can only manage to get a small luggage carrier. But a luggage carrier is just another thing to hassle with and they break easily and we're planning a hassle-free trip, aren't we? Sturdy built-in wheels and a strong suitcase leads to autonomy and basic safety and the shoulder strap on Delsey was recently replaced with a pull our handle. This isn't an item to skimp on. A cheap suitcase might break and getting it repaired could be difficult if not impossible. So start right by buying a good suitcase.

Only a few airlines won't allow carry-on luggage weighing twenty-six pounds, so you can usually get by with it even if it is a little over what's normally permitted. Always carry it as if it weighed three pounds... you're less likely to be asked to check it. A large suitcase is awkward and troublesome. It might have to fit in small shuttle boats, mini transport, or tight compartments on buses and trains. I even pull mine into restaurants; it's so small it doesn't get in anyone's way. My constant companion for six months, I even nick-named it. That's a little embarrassing to share with you. Did you ever nickname an inanimate object? Well, here I am pulling this thing behind me like a sizeable dog on a leash so I said "Come on Toto, you can do it" as we went along an especially bumpy path. From then on my suitcase was Toto (as in Dorothy and Toto, ya know).

In Paris I once stayed in an economy hotel on the fifth floor of a nice little elevator-less hotel near the Arc d'Triumph. Imagine my difficulty if I had had a large, bulky suitcase. In New Caledonia I spent 2 nights in a guest house at the top of a particularly steep hill with 150 stairs and in Thailand I rode numerous little shuttle boats out to distant islands. Most small transportation vehicles can handle only carry- on size luggage. So all in all you'll be amazed at the freedom a small suitcase affords. Back-packers frequently remarked on how handy my suitcase is. Looks-wise a suitcase separates you from hippie types who generally have more trouble with customs officials. Backpackers often wish they could pull their gear on wheels like you can.

In New Zealand, Tahiti and a few European countries it's rather expensive to buy essentials such as shampoo, toothpaste, razors, etc., so check your packing list carefully. Buy everything in lightweight plastic bottles or transfer all toiletries to lightweight plastic before you leave. Don't fill them to the top however. Altitude can cause expansion and burst your container. Could you imagine? You arrive at your destination, open your suitcase, and everything has exploded! Put your plastic bottles containing liquids in plastic zip lock bags and bring a few plastic bags for wet swimsuits and shopping as well. A small travel flashlight is vital to carry in your fanny pack at all times. You never know when you'll be out after dark. Take comfortable, lightweight slacks and a waterproof windbreaker just in case it gets cold or rainy and you may want to carry the windbreaker on the plane in case the air conditioning gets too cold. A small compact umbrella is a must and make sure it's tested not to turn inside out in a blustery wind.

Dependable walking shoes is a must with sturdy lightweight rubber soles. The lighter the weight, the easier the walking. In Southeast Asia finding good, comfortable shoes in large American sizes can be difficult. I should know. With my nine and a half B's I have good understanding. So buy your shoes in the United States unless you have tiny feet. Clothing isn't difficult to buy overseas unless you're in the Eastern Bloc countries, and it's great to go home with distinctive clothes reminiscent of the countries you've explored. Southeast Asia is remarkably inexpensive so don't be concerned about purchasing anything there. In New Zealand I bought a soft lambswool sweater because it was chilly out. Years later I still wear that furry pink pullover and feel so nostalgic.

Obviously, take clothes that don't need ironing...it's impractical to carry an iron and adaptor on the trip. Do some of you actually still iron? In Asia they'll do your laundry for you including washing, ironing and starching for about twenty-five cents for slacks and shirts. Want to move there? And don't take too much make-up. Take a basic moisturizer and minimal foundation. You won't be wearing much if any foundation in hot humid countries. Why not get a tinted sunscreen- moisturizer or moisturizer-sunscreen-foundation combination? L'Oreal has one, and a #15 or higher waterproof sunscreen is extremely important... especially in Australia where the ozone layer is drastically thin. Pack a bathing suit and/or bikini. In some countries it's okay to go topless if you're so inclined, but be sure to check the religious doctrine first. In most countries they consider it immoral but thoughtless tourists do it anyway and it contributes to some countries thinking Western women are unprincipled. Why do you think Greek men are so aggressive with us? Their women stay at home and are fully clothed. And in Arab countries the women don't even show their arms or legs! And here we come bouncing down the beach with no top on! Good golly, Miss Molly.

Bring one simple dress or skirt that doesn't wrinkle, color co-ordinated to your slacks, shirts, and shoes to dress up or down, and a pair of nice shoes for dressing up in case a special occasion arises. Co-ordinate your whole wardrobe around one or two basic light colors. Not black. Black is too hot for most temperate countries. Khaki and white are nice together, but whatever you like; you'll be looking at it a lot so choose a favorite color..

People dress up more in Singapore and parts of Europe or in Australia you might want to go dancing or to the fabulous opera house. So keep this in mind. A very basic dress can be stunning with a string of pearls (fake of course... don't tempt anyone) or a silk scarf. Pack two comfortable shirts, a light-weight sweater, five pairs of panties if you wear them. I don't as they're really not necessary, but washed at night they're dry in the morning, two to three bras and two pair of thigh-high stockings and/or cotton socks.

Now, very important, wear a fanny pack around your waist about the size of a small purse. At night sleep with it under your pillow. It must never leave your sight and should remain with you constantly. Put in your valuables and difficult to replace items such as a small zoom camera (zoom is great for getting those pictures you'd feel awkward taking up close), plane ticket, passport, credit cards, and travelers checks. Buy a squarish nylon one with 2 zippered inner compartments and 1 or 2 outer velcro pockets. The compartment closest to your skin will hold your ticket, travelers checks, credit cards, money and passport. The next pocket will hold your camera, pencil flashlight, mosquito repellent, pen and post cards. The outer ones are for coins, lipstick or chapstick (SPF #15 or higher) etc. It's a good idea to purchase your pack in the United States before you leave. You can buy one at any sporting goods store or flea market. They're superb in freeing up your arms and hands and keeping your valuables safe. Put it under your pillow at night and don't even trust it with fellow travelers with whom you might be touring. This holds way more than you would want to replace. But no one knows what's in it so don't be nervous. I once carried $5,000 in a grocery sack while making antique purchases in England. No one knew but me. If it doesn't feel uncomfortable to you, you can carry a few valuables in a shoulder harness under your clothes or extra money can be carried in an ankle wallet. Carry a photocopy of your passport if you have a safe place to store the original and don't carry anything you would be devastated to lose.

Pack a thin wash cloth and thin beach towel and when placing everything in the suitcase, place it in layers without folding in sleeves or pant legs. Then simply overlap in alternating layers. This helps prevent wrinkling. Loosely roll lingerie, t-shirts, etc., and be sure clothing material is wrinkle-free. Airmail note paper and airmail envelopes, a good writing pen and a journal could be important. If you don't want to write a journal, do what I do: take a micro cassette player/recorder. It's outstanding when you're having inspirational thoughts on a train or bus that's shaking and clacking to the jungle beat, preventing writing. You may feel a bit silly speaking into a recorder while you're on public transport, people may notice, but it's a great way to put your thoughts and ideas down and an intriguing ice breaker with the natives. It's fun to hear after you return home and you can record sounds you may never hear again ... things like the rhythmic hollow-log croaking of Balinese swamp frogs, the ancient hypnotic rhythm of African church music, or the sweet lilting voices of Romanian choir children reverberating off the Transylvanian hills. Let children speak into it and play it back for them. They'll giggle a lot and you've made a friend. Keep everything lightweight and simple. If you find you're carrying something you aren't using and may not utilize in the future, send it home. Don't tote anything you don't need.

Cotton breathes and cotton panties and bras are comfortable, healthy and cool. In most beach areas cotton cloth wraps called "sarongs" are available. Wear them over your bathing suit, to lie on the beach, wear as a skirt or use as a towel or sheet. They're a lovely bargain at two to three dollars in Southeast Asia and perfect for wearing in temples. Women can't enter temples in jeans or slacks. Oh, yeah. You know what I think about that, don't you. But it's their country and their custom so I honor it. Wrap the sarong as a skirt and they'll let you in. Shorts can be frowned on away from the beach, so a sarong is an excellent solution to many problems. Used as a towel it dries quickly because it's so thin. I keep one packed in my suitcase here in the States too. If you end up in youth hostels, they don't furnish bedding, so your sarong is your sheet. In India I stayed in a few places that had dirty bed linen so guess what, I used my sarong. Surprise!

Take film and a small camera even if you're not the shutter-clicking type. You'll be surprised how much you'll remember years later from just one simple photo. Even if you have one, don't take a multi-bodied camera with three lenses, a tripod, etc. You'll regret the weight, lose time in customs checks and find that by the time you've set up, your subject has disappeared. The small new auto-focus zoom lens cameras are both compact and practical. When photographing locals or certain religious sites, ask permission unless you're far enough away that they wouldn't notice. They may be flattered or they may disapprove. Take lightweight plastic razors if you shave. Bring a small Master padlock for your suitcase and a lightweight chain to secure the suitcase to your seat on an overnight train. Make this a constant habit: lock your suitcase always. Even when you feel perfectly safe, keep it locked.

Bring an extra pair of sunglasses made of plastic or rubber so they won't easily break, toothpaste, and a small calendar (one with all the birthdays and special dates of friends back home). Band-Aids, powdered ginger, dental floss, a little sewing kit like those that are free in hotels, antiseptic powder (in humid countries scratches don't dry), nail file, coin pouch (many countries have huge coins which, by the way, are not exchangeable from one country to the next and you'll end up carrying loads of them), deodorant soap if you're going to be in a hot, muggy area, 2 extra mini-tapes for your tape recorder, extra film for your camera, contact lens supplies if applicable, a see through carrying case for cosmetics, and an extra writing pen are all items you will need. A small calculator for money conversion, just something flat, small and simple, is essential. You can buy special conversion calculators for about $15 at luggage and travel stores if you like. They're tiny and very easy to use. Take along a mini portable alarm if you need to be up early for a flight, tampons (some Third World countries don't stock them) and a small pair of scissors and fingernail clippers.

Between what you're packing and what you wear, be sure not to take or wear anything you would be shattered to lose. It would be distressing if something you love gets lost, stolen or misplaced and avoid flashing wealth in Third World countries. i.e. don't wear your Rolex watch or your diamond tiara.

Don't take perfume to Southeast Asia or Australia. It attracts mosquitoes. Even deodorant attracts mosquitoes so buy the odorless, unscented kind. And since you'll probably be eating more fruit than usual your teeth might become sensitive so you may want to pack a toothpaste made for sensitive teeth.

For mailing items home, pack a few large, non-tear, white mailing envelopes. They're easy to mail and in most countries it's more economical if a parcel weighs one kilo or less. It's cheaper than a box as well. I sent six separate parcels of one kilo each from Thailand for less than what two threes or one six kilo parcel would have cost.

I mentioned earlier the importance of checking the temperatures in various countries before you plan your trip. Find out when winter is, how cold it is, if it's the rainy season, and just how hot or cold the various seasons can be. For instance, Thailand's winter is probably 80 degrees or more. So when they say "winter," you're definitely not going to need your wool coat. And the rainy season in Southeast Asia doesn't cool things. It just magnifies the humidity. Listening to the torrential rain pound down on the hot Balinese grass roof, I awoke the next morning to the heaviest air I've ever inhaled. The blazing tropical sun was sucking all the moisture into the air and I could hardly breathe. It was like being in a steam room at the gym. In New Zealand and Australia, winter and summer are opposite ours with December being the optimal time to visit and June biting cold with blustery winds strong enough to turn your umbrella inside out.. . Global Assist will furnish weather information or call Air Brokers International at 1(800) 883-3273 for a brochure.

Carry six to eight passport size pictures of yourself for visas, tickets and various other necessities. Those machines that pop them out for $2 are fine. Carry them in an envelope with your passport. Label your luggage inside and out with your name, address, and phone number and don't forget to include "U.S.A." Use your business address or business phone number as opposed to your home phone or home address in the event of anything unforeseen.

Packing lightweight thin material such as polyester cotton blends and washable silks that don't need ironing is germaine for hot climates. Being cool and comfortable is the number one requirement when it comes to clothing. Moist towelettes are refreshing both on the plane and in humid countries so keep a few tucked in your pocket.

Travel light and you can sing in the robber's face."
Juvenal

Packing Check List

__Toothbrush

__Toothpaste

__Hairbrush

__Make-up (optional)

__Sunscreen

__Sun glasses

__Mosquito repellent

__Thin towel

__Thin washcloth

__Lightweight walking shoes

__Lightweight cotton sleep shirt

__Cotton panties (4-5)

__Bras (2-3)

__Tampons

__Shampoo & conditioner

__T-shirts or blouses

__Cotton slacks

__Skirt or dress (optional)

__Bathing suit and bikini

__Sheet or sarong (buy there?)

__Small sewing kit

__Small lock for suitcase

__ and Chain (optional)

__Credit cards

__Mini scissors

__Mail-home non tear Envelopes (option)

__Soap (fragrance free)

__Visas (if necessary)

__Calendar

__Health certificate

__Compact umbrella

__2 writing pens

__Prescription medicines

__Large fanny pack

__Nail file and clips

__Deodorant (fragrance free)

__Dental floss

__Plane ticket

__Cosmetic case

__Windbreaker (waterproof)

__Passport size photos

__International drivers license (optional)

Tickets To Paradise

"I travel not to go anywhere but to go. The great affair is to move."

-Robert Louis Stevenson

A great place to locate phenomenal, inexpensive airline tickets is in the Sunday edition of the Los Angeles Times Travel section. Search your own major local Sunday newspaper travel section to discover how many sensational bargains you can find to exotic locations. If you've never done this I guarantee it will make you drool. You might have to arrange transportation to New York or Los Angeles but the savings would still make it worth your while. "South Pacific loops" and "Around the World" ads are generally smaller in size and will be thus captioned. Or if you're a computer buff, surf the net. If not, travel agencies will surf it for you for last minute tickets at incredibly low prices for a worthwhile fee of only about five dollars. Are there any specials to places on your dream sheet? If you have more than 10 days why not combine a few countries? My favorite combination (if you haven't guessed already) is a South East Asian jaunt combining Bali, Singapore, Malaysia, and Thailand. More than a month, why not add Australia, New Zealand, India, or Hong Kong? I wouldn't necessarily recommend spending time in Hawaii if you have limited time, though you'll likely be stopping there. That's a fun trip in and of itself and since you're traveling as far as Bali, use your valuable time to explore more distant shores.

Most around-the-world and Pacific-loop tickets have a one year time limit and this is by far the wisest choice unless you have a restricted schedule. If your schedule is restricted to under two weeks you might find a package that will cost less. My most recent ticket was valid for one year and comprised ten countries. Air fare was $1299 and I added numerous other countries as I went along, mostly by train. I was lucky enough to travel for six months... an incredible, kaleidoscopic adventure. My next trip is 17 countries for $2300.

Be sure to obtain all of your airline and/or Eurail tickets before leaving the United States. If the ticket agent doesn't get them all to you before you leave, write your credit card company and advise them not to pay that particular account until you have them. Don't accept promises. There may be a 3% charge for using a credit card on these inexpensive tickets, but if the card company furnishes free flight insurance and you have the added protection of deducting a portion if you don't receive all the tickets, it's well worth the extra cost.

To avoid imposing on friends to take you to the airport, use the airport shuttle service. They'll pick you up night or day and take you directly to the airline. They're listed in the phone book yellow pages and it's cheaper than parking your car at the airport for two weeks or more. But if you're only going for a few days you might prefer the convenience of having your car readily available when you return... whatever works for you. LAX, Southern California's main airport, has shuttles driving around the circle every few minutes so when you arrive home you can go out to the street and bargain with them. I once got a ride to Long Beach for $12.

List your countries of destination putting a check mark by the ones that require visas (typically Americans don't need visas for stays less than two weeks) and ascertain which embassies are in your local area. If you live near a large city there are probably embassies nearby. Get the first couple of visas you're going to need and apply for the remainder prior to entering the country you are bound for. Companies exist that will obtain visas for you but the charge is exorbitant and it's absurd to pay when numerous countries issue visas right in the airport. American Express, The Automobile Club, or your travel broker will furnish information regarding visas. I get the first two visas I need and while I'm traveling I get the rest as I enjoy going to foreign embassies in exotic lands; it's educational.

Be sure to ask your ticket broker if your flight will be making any additional stops. It's a real loss if there's a touchdown or layover in a country you would like to have seen. Scheduling at the outset customarily avoids extra charges. If you don't ask, they may not volunteer this information. See all you can see.

Even if the Ritz Carlton is affordable, traveling on a shoestring promises lively adventure and stimulating cultural experiences not available at finer hotels. So if you're on a tight schedule, make plane but not accommodation reservations for the full route of you trip. If you have time to spare, make reservations for the first two or three locations leaving the remainder open. Remember, reservations can be changed and you never know what stimulating occurrence or fascinating display you'll run into around the next bend. I left Greece earlier than planned as a result of the Greek males' response to women alone: a gnarly, old Mykonos innkeeper pushed me on a bed and attempted to leap on me while showing me a room. Several women I've spoken with reported similar experiences in Greece. Some men just don't respect Western women. In a few countries we're considered morally loose. If you must go to Greece, stay in the YWCA in Athens where men aren't allowed and throughout the islands and the rest of Greece try to find someone to travel with. I've had three similar experiences with Greek men. Most often however, I extend rather than curtail my stay as the positive far outweighs the negative in most countries. In all countries except Greece, Kenya and Italy I would have extended my stay if it had been feasible.

Customarily airlines request your presence at the airport an hour or two before departure. When you get through customs check to see if there's an earlier flight to your destination and even if you have confirmed tickets, if there's available seating, there's ordinarily no problem transferring to the earlier flight.

Flying the major airlines of each country results in more ticket agents being available to assist you. If you purchase an Around the

World or Pacific Loop package it could be underwritten by a larger American airline and look similar to the sample itinerary included in this book with flights on lesser known airlines. I once flew Lanka Air from Sri Lanka, stopping in Switzerland and continuing through to England for $350. If reservations to your next destination are booked, place your name on the stand-by list. Then go directly to the airport and be there in person. One person traveling alone is more likely to get on a flight than if there were two or more of you. In addition, when traveling with someone, the two tend to observe the culture from a pivotal point which prevents deeper involvement in the vibrant process of cultural exploration.

A non-stop flight is obviously preferable as there's no annoying stops along the way. Direct flights are not necessarily non-stop. They can touchdown any number of times and pick up other passengers. So check to see if it's direct and if it's going to stop, where. If it does stop, are you allowed to get off and look around? A connecting flight means changing airplanes and since you only have carry-on luggage, this isn't too problematic unless your flight is late and the other flight has departed. It's best to reserve non-stop, but I routinely take what I can get to arrive earliest at my destination. Arriving early in the day takes precedence over plane landings... more time for scouting out interesting accommodations and getting settled in.

Letters From Home

"It lies with each one of us to cut with the sword of wisdom the cords of our bondage, or to remain bound."

-Paramahansa Yogananda

For receiving mail in various countries, American Express has what is called a Travelers Companion listing their offices in every country around the world, and all you must have to utilize this convenient service is an American Express card or American Express Travelers Checks. To receive your Travelers Companion, call (800) 528-4800 or for Global Assist (any travel question... 24 hours a day) dial (800) 554-2639. With the card, you can also receive money directly from your home bank. Just know your account number or have a blank check with you. Simple and safe.

Photocopies of your itinerary listing approximate dates of arrival and the address in each country where you want mail sent is a must for your family and friends if you're gone awhile. Just check the Travelers Companion to determine the closest American Express office. Paris has about ten. I recommend choosing one near a railway station or a point of interest you plan to visit, but not all American Express offices have mail desks, so confirm this before printing your itinerary. Make sure your friends allow three weeks for mail delivery or your letters could arrive after you've departed.

An International Student ID card can be acquired by taking a class at a local university or college and provides discount prices on transportation, accommodations and entrance fees in many countries... principally Europe, Egypt, Australia, New Zealand and Israel.

Bring two small, thin address books available at most Hallmark stores for about $2 each; one for all the phone numbers and addresses of friends back home and an extra one for names of people you meet along the way. You'll be meeting countless interesting people...one of many prodigious excuses for traveling solo. When alone you'll extend yourself more and when you travel again, you'll have a multitude of addresses and phone numbers from people all over the world in one specific spot. Bring this address book along the next time you travel and inflict yourself on these same *friends* again. Just joking. I'm sure they'll be *delighted* to see you again. Who wouldn't be?

If you're feeling homesick, see an American movie. It's amazing how quickly the mind switches from being in a foreign country to being back in the good ol' U.S.A. through the movie and you'll view it from the perspective of how it portrays America and Americans as well a real eye opener. Most movies in Third World countries are in English with foreign subtitles while affluent European countries dub their movies, so ask before you purchase your ticket. I accidentally went into a German speaking movie once but they were kind enough to refund my money when I realized my mistake. Also, numerous theaters throughout the world have reserved seating so purchase your ticket in advance for a better seat. And most of them have intermission breaks in the middle of the movie! What a frustrating interruption!

It feels like a loving connection to home to write postcards and letters to family and friends, and it can be a terrific time filler in restaurants while waiting for food to arrive. Be certain in developing counties that you yourself put the stamp on the letter or postcard and watch it being postmarked if at all possible. I sent 28 postcards from Nairobi and only one arrived. Occasionally people pilfer the stamps and sell them. Brazil, India, and Kenya were my only problem. Obviously, never send money in letters.

Before leaving on your trip, tell your friends, when they send you mail, to print your last name in capital letters and underline it. In some countries the last name is written first so mail can be misfiled, meaning you'll never receive it. Printing is important in that many countries have difficulty reading our cursive writing.

he safest places in Southeast Asia to mail packages from are Singapore and Hong Kong. Be on guard when mailing from less affluent countries. Don't trust "Mail It Home" packaging services. I've known people who used these services and I myself have used two. The packages arrived battered and late with items missing. Bali was one such country and a parcel sent from India didn't arrive at all. I didn't mail a package from Kenya because of the reputation (very little gets in or out). Countries I've successfully mailed from are: Australia, New Zealand, Hong Kong, Singapore, Thailand, Germany, Switzerland, England, France, Egypt, Hungary, Yugoslavia and Austria. Occasionally it's advantageous to package and mail items yourself but check regulations in each post office before wrapping as they may have special requirements. Egypt was very strict and insisted on listing and checking each individual item I sent.

Keep a log of your purchases and approximately how much you paid in dollars. This will aid not only with mailing but with customs checks as well. With customs you need only show them a list of items you have with you since the $400 per person duty-free allowance doesn't apply to items you mailed home. And if you mark a mailed package "unsolicited gift under $50," it won't be taxed at all. Used clothing sent home is also not taxed and the next $1000 is only taxed at 10%, so no big deal. But wear the piece of clothing if you want to claim it as "used"; then it really is. There's also lower tax allowances from U.S. protectorate countries. Many items aren't permitted into the U.S.: ivory, certain furs, all sea turtle products, crocodile leather, and coral. Antiques, religious items and works of art can be difficult to export too. There's something special you'd like to buy overseas, check the price here at home so you'll have a comparison and don't forget to write down sizes you'll need. Take tiny color swatches of wallpaper or paint, clothing you'd like to buy jewelry for, etc. Just snip a small piece of fabric from the inside seam or clip a bit of carpet from an obscure spot. This goes a long way in helping you decide whether to buy that lovely little broach for your Aunt's peacock blue dress or that special vase for your mauve colored foyer. If you want to buy shoes for a child, trace her little foot on a piece of paper. For a belt, wrap a piece of string around the waist. Do the same for a hat. Sizes vary from one country to another and also pay attention to the fabric, allowing for shrinkage. After my first trip to Thailand (before I knew better) my beautiful hand stitched Thai blouses all shrunk... even in a cold wash.

If you're hungry for news from home, go to the American Embassy or the American Express office. They have up-to-date papers and magazines and it's a terrific place to ask for any help you might need. They'll answer any questions you have and you're likely to meet other English speaking travelers. A few American Express offices have a nice lounge area where you can relax and read your letters from home. Some embassies also post notices of local dangers or potential problems but anything like this would usually get to you through the grapevine while you're traveling, or call Global Assist before you leave. The last time I was in Thailand I needed a Power of Attorney drawn up for personal reasons. I was given absurd prices by various lawyers in Bangkok so I went to the American Embassy where it cost $3 and was completed quickly and efficiently.

Unless you want money from your bank at home, an American Express card isn't a requirement but merely an excellent convenience. Many credit cards have the buyer's protection plan that covers loss or breakage up to 90 days after purchase and up to a particular amount. Check with the credit card company you intend to carry. A few Third World countries add 5% to the purchase price for using an American Express card, but it could be worth the extra cost if you have a billing problem. They're good at corrections... even months later. It's unnecessary to get the platinum card unless you want to impress yourself.

Itinerary

Singapore: February 16 Airlines:	American Express 01-06 Lucky Plaza, Orchard Road 304, Garuda Singapore
Bankok: February 21 Airlines:	American Express Sea Tours Co., Nepal, 965 Rama 1 Road, Royal Siam Center Rm 414 Bankok, Thailand
Nepal: March 1	American Express Yeti Travels Pvt. Ltd., Hotel Mayalu, Jamal Tole POB 76, Durbar Mary, Katmandu, Nepal
India: March 23	American Express International Banking Corp., Wenger House Connaught Place, POB 537, New Delhi, India
India: March 30	American Express International Banking, 276 Dr. Dadabhai Naoroji Rd. Mijithia Chambers GPDB 10154, Bombay, India
Africa: April 8	American Express Silver Spear Tours, Kenya, Consolidated House Standard St. POB 40433, Nairobi, Kenya, Kenya Airways
Egypt: April 22	American Express of Egypt Ltd. Cairo Airport, Olympic, POB 2160, Cairo, Egypt
Greece: May 1	American Express Int'l Inc. Vassilissis Sophias Ave., Athens Hilton Hotel, Athens, Greece,Yugoslav Air
Yugoslavia: May 15	American Express Atlas, Yugoslav Travel Agency, Mose Pijade II, Belgrade, Yugoslavia
Czechoslovakia: May 23	American Express Cedok Foreign Travel Div., NA Prikope 18, Prague, Czechoslovakia
Austria: May 30	American Express 5 Mozartplatz, POB 244, Strausburg, Zip A5010, Austrian Air
Germany: June 5	American Express Int'l Promenadeplatz 6, Im Bayerishen Hof, Bavaria, Munich, Germany
France: June 12	Too vast, too many offices Lufthansa Air and Air France
England:: June 16	American Express Travel c/o British Airways, TWA, 421 Oxford Street, London, England.

The above is an approximation of the dates I will be in various countries and the airlines I'll be on. These dates will likely be altered so watch the dates on my post cards to you. American Express will hold letters for six weeks so not to worry, but mail letters three weeks in advance. There's no need to go to the post office when you write me. Just put two postage stamps on if it's a normal letter, print and underline my last name, and drop it in a mailbox. Also capitalize and underline the country. Don't forget to put "U.S.A." on your return address.

Shopping With Perspective

"We don't take a trip. It takes us."

-John Steinbeck

In Southeast Asia and many less affluent countries, the name of the game, believe it or not, is bargaining. When you're shopping, unless you're in a fixed price store where the prices truly are fixed, haggle. They take pleasure in it. In markets, handicraft stalls or even before climbing on transport, barter. The secret is to make a game of it. Make the first offer quite low and come up slowly. Laugh and be good humored. Have fun doing it and if you don't enjoy negotiating, frequent fixed price stores where you'll know exactly what you're getting for your money. Or check fixed price stores first to aid you in bargaining at stalls later.

If you plan to shop in numerous countries, one fun place to find sensational bargains is at the flea market. Even Java has one. You can often discover items not available in shops such as antiques at rock bottom prices, fine old lace, marionettes, exotic masks, toys, hand made items and more. I bought a stunning pearl necklace in Vienna, antique postcard albums in England, rubber sunglasses in Hawaii, a beautiful 1898 tapestry in Budapest, a gold-leaf teapot in Macau, antique spoons in Ireland, unique hand-made shoes in Nepal, and the list goes on...all at flea markets which are sometimes called Sunday markets, night markets, boot fairs, etc. depending on the country, and all for a pittance. Generally night markets serve food as well.

Western civilization brings its own form of pollution to some foreign countries, greed being foremost in my mind currently. Thus it can be found in most major cities... begging and pushing to sell to the point of annoyance. This is more true of tourist areas, so if you want to escape, go to more remote spots. And be sure when a merchant quotes a price that you know approximately how much you want to spend. If you begin bargaining, it's assumed you're going to buy. They'll probably quote double or more what an item is actually worth. Ditto for Mexico. In Bali I spotted a puppet I knew cost approximately 5,000 rupia. Asking the proprietor the price, he stated "29." I thought he meant 2,900 which would have been a steal, but he meant 29,000. When I paid him we both realized we were talking about two different amounts. Explaining good-humoredly that I knew they sold for 5,000 he laughed and said "okay, okay" and sold it to me for a fair price. So know the value and be friendly. Or if you simply know it would be a good buy in the U. S. and you like it, why not buy it anyway. If it feels like a win-win situation at the quoted price, it probably is.

Don't offer money when you take someone's picture; it establishes an attitude of envy and greed, not only in children but adults as well. It's just another form of pollution we create in developing countries. And don't tip if it's not their custom. Observe and comply with customs. If you don't know, ask. Money's great but tossing it around in foreign countries is naive, indiscreet and short sighted. You can cause grievous harm to a developing country through material indiscretion.

Surprisingly, for clothing fashions at affordable prices, I recommend Singapore and Germany. I found Paris absurdly expensive and in many haute couture shops, upon close scrutiny, little tags that said "Made in Japan" could be found. Actually, Japanese products are more affordable in America. But in Paris? Everything in Paris is expensive. I didn't find anything to be a bargain except food...superbly delicious escargot, Coquille St. Jacques, crepes, and cuisine in general, not to mention exquisite full bodied, rich red wine. It's fun just walking around Paris, seeing the Eiffel Tower and strolling the Champs Elysees. Hop on a boat and sight-see the River Seine. It's fascinating to hear about the myriad places of interest from breathtaking cathedrals to musty caves. And flea markets in Paris and all over Europe can be an entertaining way to spend a day.

Everything's relatively inexpensive in India and incredibly fine jewelry, silk, spices, trinkets, knick knacks, and painted leather are plentiful. There's a large selection of leather sandals and lovely vibrant saris. In the Northern lakes district of Kashmir (best gotten to by plane), stay on an ornate houseboat where tradesmen in row boats bring their wares of saffron, richly colored cashmere scarves and robes, elk skin gloves, jewelry, arts and crafts right to your door. I stayed on the richly appointed Mona Lisa for under $13 a night including meals and afternoon tea. Treated like a queen...it's a luxurious not to be missed experience unless they're still enduring internal political problems. Kashmir is predominantly hard core Muslim so don't go out alone at night.

Hong Kong, of course, is famous for shopping. Why not buy a silk, custom made suit or custom made snake skin shoes? Pick up several cloisonne' writing pens as gifts for people back home and don't miss the incredible night flea market (eat dinner here if you're brave) which includes a clanging traditional dragon parade.

Just before tax time in Germany, the Germans put dispensable items along the street for trash because they're taxed for every household item. It's akin to a free garage sale. Though how much is worth sending home only you can judge. I like the brocade purses and cuckoo clocks, toy cars, and music boxes, but these can't be found on the streets. Try the Sunday Market.

Be sure to ask when and where the flea markets are held...usually on weekends or at night but they can be anytime. They radiate vibrant local color and can be a marvelous learning experience... an entertaining and auspicious way to understand a country and a clever place to find outstanding bargains.

Getting it Home After You Bought it

"The time will come when people will travel in stages moved by steam engines, from one city to another, almost as fast as birds fly, fifteen or twenty miles an hour."

-Oliver Evans, 1813

With all the time invested in selecting and purchasing gifts for yourself and others, getting it all safely home is of paramount importance. Mailing parcels from Germany is expensive but safe. I paid $50 for 10 kilos and that was the least expensive way to send bulk as there is no special rates for smaller packages unless you're only sending printed material. It was actually cheaper to mail from Austria. I paid just under thirteen U.S. dollars in Austria to mail five kilos and it was extremely efficient. Buy your box at the post office or go to the nearest grocery store and get one. The post office will help you with the tape if you're polite. The paperwork wasn't as difficult as it was in Hungary or Egypt and you can purchase wonderful gifts in Germany and take them to Austria for posting. Not that Austria doesn't have its share of enticing effects. On the contrary. Spend a day at the flea market on the Danube river bank. Eat bratwurst and listen to the umpapa band play while the river glides oh so gently by.

Salzburg is an exquisite, musical city. Mozart was born here, so his home is here, as well as the Mozart Museum. Soothing classical music floats everywhere in the crisp Bavarian air. The whole of Bavaria is just breathtaking with majestic mountains, translucent lakes and awe-inspiring architecture.

In England I purchased an extra suitcase. It's so close to home I thought I would take two suitcases on the plane rather than spend money on postage for a parcel. Inexpensive suitcases are available at Petticoat Lane, which is mainly all new products these days. It used to be an antique flea market but has turned into something like the California Orange County Swap Meet with new items and too many people. So I went to Bricklane (within walking distance) and found old lace, books and pottery. Several years ago I purchased whole container loads of antiques for shipping to the U. S., but today it's harder to locate exceptional bargains anywhere in Europe.

In Vienna, you can purchase lovely brocaded material and lace curtains for your windows on the upper floor of larger department stores, particularly the stores that are away from the main tourist area. Hop on a tram and go a few blocks out of the city where you'll find local stores with decent prices. These tend to be priced in all countries more for the locals because tourists don't very often buy material and window curtains. I recommend it in England, Germany and Austria with Austria being especially promising. Do you like Austrian lace?

Mailing from Thailand is easy and there's an extensive availability of affordable merchandise, jewelry and silk in particular. Send "registered" mail only. It's just a few cents more and it's safer. Bali isn't a good country to mail from, but jewelry is exquisite, inexpensive and easy to carry in your suitcase. Singapore is absolutely super, very safe, fast and efficient. So if you buy anything in Malaysia or Bali you might want to mail from Singapore, or if you're going through Malaysia from Singapore you might want to mail in Thailand where they'll pack items for mailing for 25 baht ($1) each parcel. In Singapore you must pack it yourself, but everything is easily available: a box from the grocery store and tape at the stationary store. I think it's the safest country in Asia from which to mail packages. Mailing from India is chancy, Africa is a definite "no." Greece, Hungary, and Egypt were O.K., with Egypt and Hungary being complicated. Hong Kong is reliable but getting a box and tape can be a problem. Maybe when you're making a fairly lavish purchase (Hong Kong is known as the shopper's paradise) you could request a box at the store where you're shopping. I normally send "sea mail" unless airmail is reasonable. In Greece air mail and sea mail were about the same price so of course I chose airmail. Sea mail can take 2-3 months but if you're going to be traveling that long, who cares. It's also rather fun to receive packages after arriving home. Religious items can't be taken out of Thailand and ivory, sea turtle products, and endangered animal products won't be allowed to enter the U. S. so don't mail anything questionable unless you're willing to chance having it confiscated. You might also be fined and at the same time be contributing to the slaughtering of endangered species.

Jumping In With Both Feet

"Is there anything as horrible as STARTING on a trip? Once you're off, that's all right, but the last moments are earthquake and convulsion, and the feeling that you are a snail being pulled off your rock."

-Anne Morrow Lindbergh

Cut or perm your hair prior to leaving. It's an endeavor in frustration locating a qualified hair dresser overseas. My hair was extremely straight on my latest trip. I got bored and had it permed in Java and it remained severely damaged for months. If your hair is long, wearing it in a ponytail, braid or chignon will keep it off your neck. Battery powered curling irons and blow dryers exist but why bother with the extra weight? Arrange your hair as simply as possible so you don't need to fuss with it. You're not in a beauty pageant. If you get a shampoo and set in Southeast Asia, it's inexpensive (about $4) and includes a wonderfully relaxing head and shoulder massage. In England I had my hair colored with a wash-out tint that didn't wash out for months. It was supposed to be chestnut brown but ended up purple. And in London I got a cut that made me cry. It looked like a lawn mower had run over my head. And be sure the salon looks clean.

Traveling for two or more months you might want to hire someone to care for your mail, home, bills and anything unforeseen. If you have a secretary at work or know someone inclined to do this for a ominal charge, a reliable friend or relative, I recommend it. Have them water your plants, feed and play with your pets and do a general house check. If it's feasible to rent out your home, it's financially astute. Notify your neighbors of how long you'll be gone. Leave a key with them and put your valuables in a safe deposit box. Stop all deliveries including mail unless someone is picking it up for you. The post office will hold your mail until you get back home if you wish. Lock doors and windows and put lights and a radio on an automatic timer.

Try to schedule your departure date for a time when you aren't out of sorts with PMS. Your trip will begin on a more efficacious note if you're in a positive frame of mind. Take extra B vitamins to relieve stress and B6 in particular to relieve PMS. Start these two months before leaving if you don't take them regularly now. And don't forget the folic acid and melatonin for jet lag.

I realize what I'm asking may sound tedious but it's important for a successful trip. It's worth every minute of everything you do in preparation for this splendid journey you're taking, this scintillating adventure with life. When you travel on your own, there's such a sensation of intense accomplishment, a feeling of vibrant expansion, and an affinity for the world. Once you begin, I guarantee you will not want to stop. There's so much to experience, appreciate and learn that you'll be forever enchanted. The more you sample and achieve, the more you'll realize you've just scratched the surface. I've been around the world three times, to Southeast Asia three times, made South Pacific loops twice, Nepal, Brazil, India, Sri Lanka, and Africa once, Europe five times and I'm just beginning. I've barely scratched the surface. I'm sorry this book doesn't cover more of South America. Lots of women go there and one day I will but for economy and safety it's very hard to beat South East Asia.

There are two essential documents and a number worth serious consideration: a passport and a health certificate. Your local federal office building or post office will issue a passport (don't forget to take your photos and birth certificate) and your local health department can issue the health certificate. Write your passport number and your airline ticket numbers down and place this paper in a separate location from the originals, or make photocopies. Airlines won't issue replacement tickets unless you give them serial numbers of the one you lost and even then there's a 120 day wait period for them to see if the ticket gets used. So besides your passport number, have your airline ticket numbers and traveler checks numbers stored in a separate location. Give a copy to a trusted relative or friend at home so you can call them for the information if necessary. If your passport is lost or stolen, report it to the local police and to the American Embassy where they can usually issue a new one within 24 hours. If you plan to drive abroad, get an international driving permit from the local Automobile Club. It costs about $5 and is valid for a year. A test isn't required nor is membership in the Automobile Club. Just bring two passport size photos. It's easier to rent a motorcycle if you have an international driving permit and a must for renting a car. In Bali it's difficult to rent a motorcycle and I don't recommend it; it's dangerous. But I've rented motorcycles and mopeds in Thailand and the Greek Islands for wonderfully picturesque seashore and mountain rides.

A few things to consider before you leave: if it's tax time, be sure to square up before leaving or file for an extension. If you own property, arrange to pay the property tax when it's due. As for your car, disconnect the battery if you're going to be gone for an extended period of time... a piece of cake even if you're mechanically clueless. Park it in a garage or cover it and lower the insurance premium to a bare minimum so you don't have that unnecessary expense. I'm selling my car prior to leaving and will purchase another upon my return. Should you elect to do this as well, retain your liability insurance as a stiff penalty is assessed if you don't. Silly, huh.

If your bank has American Express travelers checks, buy them. The American Express offices will only cash their own, but do shop around for cashing in foreign countries. Compare various rates and charges and ask if there's a fee to you for cashing. Probably the worst place to cash travelers checks is major hotels and airports, although in India this is the best place. Enquire of other travelers as to who has the prime rates. Most travelers know. I learn within a day of arriving because I shop around. I stroll the streets checking rates that are posted in bank windows and exchange houses. Especially in this day of the fluctuating dollar, obtain the most for your money. If you have a Visa or MasterCard, bring them. I was concerned about being properly billed, being away so long, and in fact, in Cairo a bill was misread by American Express (with good reason) and my account overcharged by $200. I telephoned when

I arrived home three months later and it was instantly corrected. Visa is also widely accepted and I've never had a problem. Just be certain your assistant at home is paying in a timely manner to retain your good credit rating.

What Are You Waiting For?

"One of the illusions of life is to continue to live helplessly. As soon as you say "It's no use", it becomes so . . . to think you cannot change at will is delusion."

-Paramahansa Yogananda

Shaktie Gawane in her book, Visualizations, states "every moment is a moment of creation, and each moment of creation contains infinite possibilities. I can do things the way I have always done them or I can look at all the other alternatives and try something new and different and potentially more rewarding. Every moment presents a new opportunity and a new decision." What a wonderful opportunity to create something fresh and new in your life, something exciting, enlightening, and revealing ; perhaps more than you've ever allowed yourself before. Now is the time to begin. If you aren't doing things on your own, why not practice? Go to a movie by yourself or eat out alone . . . although I must say that eating alone in one's hometown isn't nearly as colorful as dining in an exotic port. At home it can feel a bit reclusive. In an exotic port it feels free and sophisticated. Write post cards, read a book, or just relax and enjoy the unique ambience while waiting for your food. In most outdoor cafes they sort of expect you to eat alone. The point is to begin. Take action.

I often allude in this book to getting sick, safety, immunizations, and all of the potential difficulties because this is pertinent information, but this need not be your reality. Your reality is created by you to be anything you desire. This excursion can be blissful acknowledgment of your self and the world. Recognize the divinity in all people, contemplate humankind with her many, diverse cultures and distinctive civilizations. You'll savor this breathtaking adventure, this sensational undertaking, and yearn to encounter more. Facing new challenges is inspiring and exhilarating . Conquering them is a thrill you can only experience by pushing out the boundaries and stretching beyond your own limits. Each person's mind holds all the chains of bondage as well as the keys to freedom. Extend your periphery with yourself and nature. Traveling solitary is liberating, and can bring you face to face with your own most autonomous and radiant self.

I've only scratched the surface and given you the tiniest sample of what is possible. Each expedition is as matchless as a delicate snowflake. My heart travels with you, knowing your individual journey will be the delight of a lifetime. My wish for you is to be enveloped in new found strength, joyous solitary adventures in life, and the courage to be all you are and more. For, *Whether you think you can or think you can't, you're right.*——Henry Ford

Think as Saadi thought, "Roam abroad in the world and take thy fill of its enjoyment before the day shall come when thou must quit it for good." And finally, a bit of advice from Erma Bombeck, "Get off your cusp and live."

Bon Voyage.

All My Love,

Shalla

Letters:

LETTER FROM HUNGARY 1989
(only months before the fall of Communism in the Eastern Bloc)

Dear Ones,

I'm on a train leaving Budapest, Hungary headed back to Belgrade, Yugoslavia having spent three weeks in Romania and Hungary with very wonderful families. The Romanian experience was heart wrenching and educational and could change a person's political persuasion.

I had to guard what I wrote in Romania because they censure the mail (so you may not receive the post cards I sent). Groceries are purchased with stamps, like during World War II, with each person only allowed so much bread and so much meat (one kilo a month). Gas is the same. If they're rich enough and lucky enough to have a car (most are pieces of junk because only Romanian cars are allowed), or if they had another kind before Romania over took that part of Hungary they can't get parts. They're only allowed 15 liters of gas per month . . . enough for about 200 miles.

I stood in a half hour line to buy ice cream that tasted so awful I threw it in the trash. Going in grocery stores and department stores is a depressing experience as you see exactly the same thing in every store and very little at that. In book stores they can only buy books about "our great and wonderful leader" or art books. TV is on two hours a day, one channel, and is usually poems about "our great and wonderful leader and country." If they have a TV and sell it then they must go to the police station during the two hours to hear the songs and/or poems of "our great and wonderful leader." The Hungarians and Romanians are trapped by this fanatical dictator, and Communism.

It's against the law for citizens of Romania to let anyone spend the night with them so they had to hide me and when I was near police (and they are EVERYWHERE with machine guns) I didn't speak so they wouldn't know I'm foreign. I smuggled in fruit, meat, butter, shoes, coffee, toys, medicine, and cigarettes (for bribes), and was lucky. The border guards took nothing from me . . . except money and cigarettes. The children, who have never tasted oranges in their lives, ate the oranges like they were hot fudge sundaes. The juice dripped down their little chins and their eyes sparkled.

People cried when I left. I represented Hajnel (my travel friend and their sister, daughter, Mother, friend) but, more, I represented freedom... America... the freest country in the world... while they suffer in their Communistic perdition. No one is free to make money, to travel, to enjoy anything other than just what the government allows, which isn't much.

I sat at the border crossing for three hours at midnight and they dragged the lady sitting next to me off the train and another one started sobbing uncontrollably. One man told me they took all his clothes.

A man just came by selling coke and beer. It cost 7,500 dinar ($.50). Oh how good to be in Yugoslavia (the freest of the communist countries). And here in Yugoslavia this letter won't be censured. The food is good and there is more variety of things to buy. But even here communism has it's crippling effect and the people are mostly very poor. I would like to meet someone who lives here and speaks English to ask how they feel about the government and the effects of communism on their country, to see if they detest it as much as the other countries do.

I feel so spoiled and lucky. Even before this trip though I felt spoiled and fortunate to have such wonderful friends and daughters.
I miss and love you all. I hope things are going well at home. It's difficult to call (in Hungary I waited over two hours to call Debi on her birthday and then got a recording.)

All my love,

Shalla

Notes From Near & Far

BALI:

Hi Girls.

I hope this finds you both well and happy. I'm lying on my bed in my beach bungalow looking out at the crystal aquamarine waves crashing against a sandy palm lined shore. It's 7:30am, roosters are crowing and my stomach is growling from the aroma of sizzling bacon and freshly brewed coffee wafting thru the tropical morning air.

I'm leaving this village today for one further up the road to gain a change of scenery and a bungalow with softer beds. This one's $2 including breakfast. Guess I'll have to find a high class extravagant one for $4 to get a softer bed.

Dinner last night was a bang out all-you-can-eat buffet consisting of juicy roast pork in garlic sauce, crispy sweet and sour duck, fish satay with creamy peanut sauce, crunchy tossed green salad, rice, peas and coconut salad, and fresh fruit of every description for desert. Not bad for $2 huh? I ordered mango juice to drink and they brought me 10oz. of pureed mango for 35 cents...not exactly thirst quenching, but pretty darn delicious all the same.

Pam, I'm really using the trip calculator you got me a LOT...many times a day in fact. I punch in "calc," then "price", then "compute" and it gives me the U. S. dollar price of everything. It will really come in handy in Singapore too, when I want to call home . . . to know what time it is there. Right now it's 3:40pm February 6th where you are (because I'm over the International Date line I'm a day ahead). I wonder what you're both doing. Cheryl's probably working at the hospital and Pam's probably at school. Or is it Sunday? If it's Sunday Cheryl's probably at Rich's and Pam's probably delivering pizzas.

I feel a bit lonely thinking of you but I haven't eaten breakfast so that will help pick me up. Balinese coffee really gives me a rush. It's nearly black and always has coffee grounds in the bottom of the glass since they don't use filters (they serve it in glasses) and if you ask for milk or cream in most Asian countries you get sweetened condensed milk. And you know how I love that but in COFFEE? I don't think so. I sure love you guys and can't wait to call you from Singapore to hear your voices.

All My Love Always,

Mom

INDIA:

Hi Darling.

Happy birthday. Boy have I been buying you some fantastic birthday presents . . . amethyst ear rings, an intricate gold and silver ring, and 2 unique horses for your collection, one wood and copper, one polished stone.

I'm staying on a house boat in Kashmir, furnished with ornate English antiques, exquisite old carpets, heavy brocade draperies and hand carved ceilings and walls. It's altogether breathtaking and at only $13 a night including meals, quite a bargain. The silvery lake reflects the majestic snow capped mountains in the back ground and combined with the archaic wooden structures of the city, creates an incredibly picturesque adventure of exotic proportions. I'm so glad you were born.

All my love on your birthday and always,

Mom

NEPAL:

Hi Girls!

I'm in Nepal and the crisp, clear Fall day feels exhilarating after Thailands' sultry tropical heat. But Nepals' poverty jumps up and knocks me in the face. Do people bathe here? And the drug scene and black market for money are absolutely amazing.

In Kathmandu everything is dun colored except the vibrant tourist items hanging in limited supply in store fronts. But the food is good when it doesn't make me sick, jewelry and clothes are inexpensive and rick shaws will take me around town for a pittance or I rent bikes for $1.50 a day. So the dusty brown poverty against a backdrop of breathtaking mountains and azure skies creates a fascinating contrast. I'm sitting at a quaint outdoor cafe eating a bowl of porridge and yak butter. There's bugs in the salt. Write me. I miss you.

Love U,

Shalla

AUSTRIA:

Hi Sweetie.

Here I am in Vienna and I could dress fabulously here if I had a million dollars tucked in my money belt. Everything is SO expensive in comparison to where I've been. Guess this is the end of the economical part of my trip but I am saving here and there by eating soup and frequenting McDonalds. Can you imagine me in McDonalds?? Actually it's quite tasty here and the Austrians seem to really enjoy it. I think most countries around the world love McDonalds! Hajnel insisted on walking a mile or so to eat at one in Belgrade. And it's definitely a big deal in Third World countries. But back to lovely Vienna, you know how I love to shop so I will miss the inexpensive countries. Vienna does have a fabulous flea market though. . . right on the river bank. I saw Dangerous Liaisons at an elegant theater last night. Unfortunately it wasn't in English.

All my love,

Mom

JAVA:

Dear Cheryl,

I'm drinking watermelon juice and waiting for my $1.76 lunch of mouth-watering vegetable soup, fried rice and coconut, and cookies. My hotel room is $8.23 a night including breakfast and afternoon tea and cookies. It has a sit down toilet (unusual for this part of the world), a shower, sink, front patio and exquisite tropical garden area off the sparkling pool. I'm sitting by the pool watching a guy play with a monkey. I'm not sure which one has the biggest brain; I think I'd put my money on the monkey. And speaking of monkey brains, I'm not sure if today's the 11th or 12th but it's definitely Sunday and I'm so hungry for word from home as there's not an American Express office here, and I haven't been able to mail anything out for 8 days. I miss you and love you lots.

Mom

YUGOSLAVIA:

Dearest Pam,

Prague is fantastically beautiful with statues and ornamentation on every building, cobblestone streets, friendly people and decent food. You'd love it. I do.

I may fly back to Romania to smuggle more food to the people I left pieces of my heart with but I've been away from home so long, I feel torn. How's school? I hope you're enjoying your classes. I know sometimes it must feel monotonous but you're creating such a meaningful future. I'm proud of all your efforts.

All my love always,

Mom

INDIA:

Hi Mom & Dad.

This post card is an actual photo of my house boat Mona Lisa on the Dal Lake in Kashmir. Mr. Sultan and his family of 2 sons and 11 daughters own and run it and I'm being treated like a queen. Mr. Sultan's son escorts me and the other woman who's staying on the boat, into town...for safety. A war may be eminent between the Islamic Kashmiris and democratic India. I personally went through two strict searches just to come here. They don't want people smuggling in guns. Kashmir is Muslim while most of India is Hindu so Islamic Kashmiris want to be part of Pakistan for that reason. India is very disconcerted that the USA is backing Kashmir and Pakistan. They feel if we were true to what we espouse we would back a democratic society. It's illuminating when traveling what gets discovered or uncovered; I had no idea we were backing Pakistan or even that this was happening.

I bought Dad a lovely cashmere scarf from a salesman, one of many who come up to the houseboats in canoes. It's like a whole city of houseboats lined up along the far shore of the lake and it goes on for miles with long distinctive house boats of various description and quality. Price wise it isn't as economical as Thailand but it's fascinating and beautiful even in it's dire poverty.

Miss you, Love,

Shalla

GREECE::

Hi Everyone.

I'm on Mykonos Island of Jackie and Aristotle fame but will leave in a few days via ferry to a nearby island as Mykonos is very expensive. Lovely narrow winding streets, wind mills and haute couture shops abound.

I rented a Moped on Peros for $5 and rode along winding narrow streets through flower strewn fields and quaint villages, managing to cover the whole gorgeous island in a day. Ate lunch at a charming little fishing village...fish, olives, feta cheese and wine. On these islands I generally go into the kitchen and select from large pans of food that they've prepared for that day; mostly delicious, in contrast to the food I had in Athens which was mostly greasy and inedible. But remember I'm traveling on a shoestring so I'm not frequenting 5 star restaurants.

All my Love,

Shalla

YUGOSLAVIA:

Dear Mom and Dad,

I'm in Bar, Yugoslavia traveling with a Romanian girl who's dragging around a TON of luggage. We're on our way to Dubrovnik and then on to Hungary by train.

Belgrade is just lovely with lots of gorgeous parks, towering trees and magnificent old architecture. They have a McDonalds and it's all decorated in pink marble and plants. They seem very proud of this one bit of Western civilization.

The food's delicious and wine is cheap. It's Easter here (Orthodox) so everything is closed for 4 days. Consequently I can't check American Express for mail from you.

Love You,

Shalla

THAILAND:

Hi Mom & Dad.

I'm in Thailand and feeling better. I'm a little weak from the Bali flu but my head is less congested and I can hear better. I'm on a beautiful little island off the Southern coast sitting at an outdoor cafe waiting for my breakfast of fruit salad and porridge. The coffee is rich and strong. The Thais tell me I'm beautiful. Interesting. They seem very open with their feelings and their women are considered some of the most beautiful in the world so having them think I'm pretty is incredibly flattering. But these islands are what's beautiful; just breath-taking..

Miss you, Love,

Shalla

P.S. Dad, did you get the birthday card I sent?

INDIA:

Hi Darlin'.

I'm sitting on the top floor of the fabulous Taj Mahal Hotel in Bombay pigging out on a gourmet buffet for 125 rupia ($7 US) and staying at the YWCA sharing a room with a woman from Sierra Leone. The Y is very old and stately. It's located on a tree lined street, sparsely furnished, quiet and clean. I especially like Y's because they're safe and quiet. And most of them furnish food...at least breakfast.

From Delhi it took 28 hours by train to reach Bombay on a sleeper train for women; a very absorbing experience. Write me.

Love,

Mom

ROMANIA::

Loved Ones,

I'm in beautiful forested Transylvania, Romania and leave in a few days for Budapest. I'm a bit off the beaten path but there are reasons that I can't mention in this post card. I will explain later. I'm having a truly incredible adventure and enjoying the people and country immensely. Very different from home.

Love and kisses,

Shalla

INDONESIA:

Dearest Debi,

The Cameron Highlands in Central Malaysia are rich with verdant jungles and tropical rain forests, not to be missed. There's a sizable Indian population so I dine primarily on typically Indian cuisine. I saw a movie last night in a small local building since they don't have theaters. Turned out I had seen it before as they get movies 6 or more months after us and in these little villages it's more like a year .I will leave shortly to venture further North. Kuala Lumpur was extraordinarily beautiful with lots to see and do. Can't wait to see Jack and Glad in Thailand. How's Gucci? Write me.

All my love,

Mom

BALI:

Dear Mom and Dad,

Sitting under a multi-colored flowering tree at an outdoor cafe in Bali, a sumptuous buffet is being prepared at $2.05 per person. The food here is so delicious and I'm eating mostly fruit and vegetables. I eat papaya for the vitamins (you know I don't like it). I get no news of the outside world here so if you need to know something to write to me about, tell me what's happening in the world.

Love you,

Your Daughter

YUGOSLAVIA:

Hi Everyone.

Here I am in Yugoslavia traveling with a Romanian girl who's defecting. I may go to Romania to see her husband and child.

I love Yugoslavia. It's beautiful and inexpensive and feels so good to be away from Greek men and greasy Greek food (I have some tales to tell you), although I loved the islands.

I'm in Dubrovnik right now waiting for the train to Belgrade. Can't wait for news from home.

LOVE YOU. Shalla

GERMANY:

Dear Mom and Dad,

I'm in Heppenheim, Germany staying with a very nice girl I met biking in Nepal. We went to a wine-fest Friday and yesterday we drove to Heidelberg (30 K away). Germany's so beautiful and I'm having a fabulous time. In Austria I went to a Mozart Exposition and visited his birthplace; it was sooo great. I feel blessed.

I may skip Italy and Greece since I've "been there, done that" and go straight to Istanbul...playing it by ear. By the way, I dyed my hair red in Vienna and I think it looks pretty good . . . a fun change from brown. I thought I should tell you so you won't be shocked when you see me. I may be back home for Cheryl's birthday.

Hugs and Kisses,

Shalla

EGYPT:

Dearest Daughters,

So sorry I'm not getting more postcards off to you but some places are more difficult to mail from than others.

I'm in Luxor, Egypt traveling with an American girl from Diamond Bar I met at the Cairo Airport. She said when we met she was saying a prayer that she wouldn't have to travel alone in Egypt. I think it's the first time I've been the answer to someones prayer.

The hot Sahara sun parches my skin and dust chokes my throat. The Nile is small and unswimmable for health reasons. Horses trod down the road along with camels, donkeys and buses but it's truly a fabulous ancient place with eerie tombs and astonishing pyramids. I ride a bike all over Luxor which use to be the capitol . And the Cairo Museum is incredible. I leave for Jerusalem tonight. MISS YOU.

Love you.

Mom

GREECE:

Dear Mom & Dad,

Arrived in Athens at 11:30 on the 20th and got your letter dated April 2nd. Traveling with a spunky 85 year old lady from San Clemente, California. Staying at the YWCA near Central Park. Athens is a big change from the camels and donkeys in Egypt. I ride the trolley-type buses all over town. Food is greasy, weather's beautiful and I'm taking a ferry out to the Islands.

Love you,

Shalla

GREECE

Hi Guys.

I'm on a 12 hour overnight ferry ride to Santorini Island with a lovely little 70 year old Australian lady with a backpack.

Greece is not cheap; I've been shopping for 2 days (and exploring) and have only purchased food.

Had a rich Greek following me all over Athens yesterday offering to buy me jewelry or give me money . I think he thought I was a "working girl" . I finally managed to give him the slip by going in the YWCA but not until I was ready to drop. Each time I lost him he reappeared. I now understand Jackie; she probably got tired of running. What is it they say about persistence?

Love you,

Shalla

KENYA:

Hi Guys.

Well it takes about an hour of standing in line to mail anything here so if you don't hear from me a lot you'll know why.

Nairobi is a very modern city with lots of high rises. Not quite what I expected. Safaris are terribly expensive and some people scare me. It's not safe to go out at night or to cross the park alone. The food has a distinct British flair and I will leave as soon as I get my passport back from the Egyptian Embassy where I'm getting my visa.

I went to a place called Tree Tops (a type of safari) and it was fabulous to see the myriad of animals and to stay at such a unique hotel set in the top of trees, but it topped out my budget. How are things at home? Wish you were here . . . or maybe not... for your sake.

All my love,

Shalla

NEPAL:

Dear Debi,

Here I am in Nepal trying to stay well but, like all the other tourists, losing the battle more often than not.

I think this is the dirtiest place I've been in my life but India lies just ahead on my agenda and it's rumored to be worse, so we'll see. Even in squalor there can be something compelling and intrigueing but at the moment it escapes me.

Here in Nepal the people look you right in the eye and lie and rip you off while swearing on their mothers' grave they're telling the truth... so that's nice. If I really want to know something I ask about 4 people and do a consensus. What an education!

Love You,

Mom

NEPAL:

Hi Sweetie.

They have yaks here. Did you eat yak meat in Peru? Yak butter is great, isn't it. Nepal itself is a pit though. Engrid and I laugh a lot (between trips to the bathroom). We went on a safari last week; a horrendously uncomfortable bus ride to an ox cart, across rivers to the safari camp which could have been better. It was educational though.

Love you lots.

Mom

About The Author

Shalla Callahan is a single female who, against tremendous odds, raised four daughters alone on a modest income with little assistance. Over the past 30 years she worked, attended school, made a home for her daughters and traveled extensively. While earning a degree in psychology and raising her daughters, Shalla set up and ran her own house cleaning business, painted portraits, managed apartment buildings, modeled clothing, worked in real estate, and was the senior partner in her own antique import business.

Shalla completed her first solo around the world trip in 1975. Subsequent trips have included Europe (five times), Kenya, Egypt, Brazil, India, Australia, New Zealand, Japan, Taiwan, Hong Kong, New Caledonia, Tahiti, Malaysia, Indonesia, Nepal, Singapore, Ireland, Scotland, England, Germany, Austria, Switzerland, Italy, Spain, France, Holland, Belgium, Hungary, Yugoslavia, Czechoslovakia, Romania, Portugal, Bahamas, Java, French West Indies, Caribbean, Mexico, Turkey, Laos, Thailand, Macau, Sri Lanka, Greece, Bali, and Morocco.

Shalla lives in a small Austrian style castle which she has been renovating and decorating for the past seven years in Long Beach, California. She enjoys sunset beach walks, biking around local historic neighborhoods, ethnic restaurants, music, theater, and replenishing spiritually at the Church of Religious Science in Huntington Beach.

In 1995 Shalla made the intellectual and philosophical decision to become a lesbian after years of frustrating attempts to partner with the opposite sex. "It only makes sense," she says, "putting men and women together can be as difficult as mating a cat with a dog. For me, it just didn't work. Being a lesbian allows me to be more powerfully myself than I've ever been before and if I had been born a soul without a body I would have gravitated toward the feminine from the beginning."

A semi-autobiographical novel of her many worldly exploits is due out next Spring.

Order Form

Callahan Castle Publishing
264 Lowena Drive
Long Beach, California 90803

Please send ______ number of books to:

Company name: ______________________________

Name: ______________________________

Address: ______________________________

City: ____________________ State: ______ Zip: _________

Telephone: (____) ____________________

Sales tax: $1.07 per book

Shipping:
Book rate: $12.95 per book
plus shipping cost of $2.00 for the first book and .75 cents for each additional book.
(Surface shipping may take three or four weeks)
Air Mail: $3.50 per book